THOMAS Y. CROWELL COMPANY
New York,N.Y. 10019

RING LARDNER AND THE PORTRAIT OF FOLLY
   Twentieth Century Writers Series
By Maxwell Geismar

"At a time when literary criticism has moved
from theory, and its dependence on every science
from anthropology to neurology... it is a
pleasure to find one of America's finest
practical 'readers' still at work. And this
appears to be precisely what Maxwell Geismar's
critical idea is: to read without the critical
encumbrances of contemporary theory blocking
his view.... Carefully selecting passages in
Lardner's work, Geismar allows us to come to
know the man he is introducing directly, and
we come to share the same enthusiasm that is
so noticeable in the critic's relationship to
the author.... we are drawn into a company of
friends, where human truths about the author
come as spontaneously as casual conversation."
Best Sellers

Ages 12 and up
Boards: $4.50

RING LARDNER
AND
THE PORTRAIT
OF FOLLY

TWENTIETH-CENTURY AMERICAN WRITERS

ERNEST HEMINGWAY
AND THE PURSUIT OF HEROISM
by Leo Gurko

RING LARDNER
AND THE PORTRAIT OF FOLLY
by Maxwell Geismar

THORNTON WILDER:
The Bright and the Dark
by M. C. Kuner

TWENTIETH-CENTURY AMERICAN WRITERS

RING LARDNER
AND
THE PORTRAIT
OF FOLLY

By Maxwell Geismar

THOMAS Y. CROWELL COMPANY

New York

ACKNOWLEDGMENTS

The author wishes to thank Charles Scribner's Sons for permission to use quotations from "Marriage Made Easy," "A Visit to the Garrisons," "Night and Day," "Dogs," "Tips on Horses," "Cora, or Fun at a Spa," and "Taxidea Americana," from *First and Last* edited by Gilbert Seldes; the preface to *The Love Nest and Other Stories*; and "Dinner" from *Round Up*. Quotations from the works of Ring Lardner are fully protected by United States and International Copyright.

Designed by Sallie Baldwin

Manufactured in the United States of America

L. C. Card 77–175105
ISBN 0–690–70234–5

1 2 3 4 5 6 7 8 9 10

For Katie, Peter and Liz

CONTENTS

EARLY LIFE
1

Ring Lardner is still known to many people as a famous sportswriter, an author of popular sketches and short stories, and a funnyman, just as Mark Twain was considered to be merely another popular entertainer of no great literary importance during his lifetime. Among the galaxy of modern American writers—such figures as Ernest Hemingway, F. Scott Fitzgerald, Thomas Wolfe, John Dos Passos, and William Faulkner, or Edith Wharton, Willa Cather, and

Ellen Glasgow—the work of Ring Lardner is still relatively unknown. Yet he occupies a special and perma-
nent place in our literary heritage, and those who
admire him sometimes admire him the most.

This is partly because Lardner had so brilliant a wit,
and was so utterly sophisticated in his humor and
comedy. Our society, including our schools and teach-
ers, possibly even more than our students, is not in-
clined to take humor seriously or to regard it as one
of the great gifts of life, perhaps the greatest. We look
upon humor, from our puritanical and our middle-class
origins alike, as something different, as something not
quite respectable, if not downright dangerous and
frightening. And perhaps that view is correct, because
once you have been caught up by the great comedy, or
the great tragicomedy, of a Mark Twain or a Ring
Lardner, you will never be quite the same again. But
you will be better and happier and more interesting, I
promise you, and see life more freshly, and you will
no longer be able to endure living your life *without*
humor.

This is a book, then, about Ring Lardner's life and
work and talent; and since his talent was so remarkable and his work is usually so funny, in a wide range
of humor from comedy and farce to devastating satire
and even surrealistic Dada, or deliberate nonsense, you
should come to Lardner relaxed and ready to enjoy
yourself. You begin reading Lardner, and sooner or
later you start laughing. Our understanding of and
admiration for the man begin then, too.

He was born in Niles, Michigan, on March 6, 1885,

the youngest of the nine children of Henry Lardner and Lena Phillips Lardner, and he was named, of all things, Ringgold Wilmer Lardner, after his father's first cousin. Young Ringgold's family were prosperous and comfortable and cultivated and happy Midwestern folk living in a fashion that is almost unknown today. Theirs was the same provincial American culture that Booth Tarkington wrote about: an old-fashioned, charming, and gracious way of family life that has almost vanished with the growth of the cities and suburbs, the scientific-industrial complex in America, the standardized and mechanized "instant" society, the cultural values of Hollywood and TV. It was from this older mid-American background, too, that Ring Lardner surveyed the Jazz Age and the Lost Generation, the boom and the bust, the Roaring Twenties and a new gilded age which he described with such a sardonic eye. This popular sportswriter and entertainer was, in fact, one of the sharpest cultural historians of that gaudy period.

Three of the six older Lardner children died in childhood. The remaining children were divided into two sets: the eldest—William, Henry, Jr., and Lena— were separated by ten years from Rex, Anna, and Ringgold. The Lardner house was on "the southern edge of the town, near the steep wooded bank of the St. Joseph River." According to Lardner's biographer, Donald Elder,

The immense yard covered a whole block of several acres and was enclosed by a rail fence. The land

sloped gently down from the eastern boundary
toward the river; behind the house were fields and
gardens, which were Mr. Lardner's special interest
—his roses were famous locally—and on the lawn in
front were tall pine trees. There were also a baseball diamond, tennis court, and a coach house with
a stable of horses. The house was dark gray stucco
with steeply gabled roofs which shone on moonlight
nights like some fairy-tale castle; and the eaves and
porches were adorned with wooden scrollwork. In
its spacious grounds it stood apart from the town,
a place of quiet charm and good taste, in an age
when ostentatious and hideous piles were being
erected on Main Street by prosperous merchants
and businessmen.

It is curious that Ring Lardner never returned to
this Midwestern scene of his childhood in his mature
work; whereas Sherwood Anderson, for example,
would spend his life remembering and examining this
vanishing American small-town existence, and in *Main
Street* and *Babbitt* Sinclair Lewis would satirize
savagely the new commercial society just then being
established in the Midwest.

Niles had its Anglo-Saxon "aristocracy" of wealth
and family and provincial culture; those in the poorer
working class were mainly German and Irish immi-
grants. Mrs. Lardner wrote poetry and short stories,
educated her children in literature, music, and the
drama—far more than most parents do now—and

though democratic in taste for that place and period, she sought to keep her children apart from the less cultivated town children—to whom young Ring soon gravitated.

Life in that earlier American scene was very different from life today. There were no automobiles, and dad did not rush off every morning to catch the 8:05 train for work. The father was still a strong influence in family life, and there was a strong family life. He usually came home for lunch from his office in town; sometimes, as in the case of prosperous, comfortable, and cultivated farmers (compared with the industrial combines of modern agriculture), his office was right there on the farm, where he raised and traded race-horses along with his herd of cattle. The Lardners were part of a town that was surrounded by such farms and which was shaped and colored by the patterns and values of an older agrarian and mercantile society.

In those days everybody in Niles knew about the doings of their neighbors; society was like a large family itself, or not too far from the communes which some young people are setting up today in order to combat a social life they feel to be hopelessly depersonalized and fragmented. It was difficult for a businessman to prosper by trickery without being caught out, and to be wealthy was also a sign of character and respectability. The pace of life was slow; people had time to be interested in each other—and what else gives real meaning to life? Life was also pretty settled and secure —or seemed so—before the First World War and the

Second, and an epoch of revolutionary change through-
out the world. Though the American South was still
in the throes of the Reconstruction period, there were
no black ghettos anywhere in the nation, no racial war-
fare. Even poverty, like the status of the so-called inferior races, was then deemed immutable, and the
cities had not yet become jungles that destroyed masses
of people. There were financial panics and depressions,
to be sure, and there were savage labor riots and armies
of unemployed men, but this was part of the new
scientific-industrial society just coming into power,
while the rest of America slumbered happily in the
idyllic garden of the past.

Until Ring was eleven, he wore a brace on his leg;
he had been born with a deformed foot which was
gradually cured, though his left leg was always somewhat thin. The real consequences of such childhood
events are always obscure; in the history of creative
talent, they can lead equally well to positive or nega-
tive effects; all we can do is to remember that they
happened. He took to his musical education with a
special enthusiasm, and this may account for what
later on became one of the most sensitive of all ears
to the American language as it is actually spoken, the
living folk language, which is quite different from the
formal or literary English most of us are taught.

He himself did not go to school until he was twelve
years old. The education he received from his mother,
and from the Lardners' own library, was better than
what he could have gotten in the public schools of the

day; and when he did enroll, he was much more advanced in knowledge and taste than most of his schoolmates. Along with music, Ring was fascinated with literature—and with baseball.

The Lardner children had a tutor for more advanced studies, and here is Ring Lardner's description of their lessons, written years later in the famous language which, "one'ct you get to know it you can't never quite get over it."

> . . . us 3 youngest members of the family was too fragile to mingle with the tough eggs from the West Side and the Dickereel. We had a private tutor that came to the house every morning at 9 and stayed till noon and on acct. of it taking him 2 and a ½ hrs. get us to stop giggling, why they was only a ½ hr. left for work and this was generally always spent on penmanship which was his passion. . . .
>
> The rules of penmanship at that time provided that you had to lean your head over to the left, wind up like they was nobody on second base, and when you finely touched pen to paper, your head followed through from left to right so that when you came to the end of the line, your right ear laid flat on the desk.

As we shall see, Ring Lardner's early "Rules of Penmanship" anticipate his rules of writing and his general view of life.

In high school Ring and his brother Rex formed a singing quartet with two friends and went around serenading the Niles girls. Ring played on the football team; he studied German; and he began to fraternize with those lower orders of society with whom he always felt more at home, who furnished so much of his later literary material, and whom he described perhaps more accurately and more hilariously than any other writer of his time.

By 1901, the year that Ring graduated from the Niles High School, the Lardner family fortune, based mainly on Western land mortgages, had collapsed. Ring's brother Rex had gone to the University of Michigan, but Ring does not seem to have been interested in college; he had but one ambition—to become a baseball reporter. He was a tall, solemn, shy boy, with immense dark eyes, and the baseball players of that day recalled that it was impossible to make him laugh. Before becoming a sportswriter he had the usual variety of jobs that adolescents pick up; he attended Armour Institute in Chicago; he returned home to Niles for a while. He was a reporter for various small-town papers and then for the *South Bend* (Indiana) *Times*.

In the summer of 1907 he met Miss Ellis Abbott of Goshen, Indiana, whom he was to court for four years, while he tried to make his way in the newspaper world. That same year he became a full-fledged baseball reporter on the Chicago *Inter-Ocean*. One of his friends has stated that at twenty-two he "looked like Rameses II with his wrappings off"—Rameses II being a well-known Egyptian pharaoh, who is also one of the best preserved through mummification. He was dark complexioned, and once, later on, he told a Southern acquaintance that he had been born of poor but respectable colored parents.

He began to associate with the more celebrated sportswriters, including such figures as Hugh Fullerton, Walter Eckersall, and Hugh E. Keogh—the "Hek" of the Chicago *Tribune*'s famous column, "In the Wake of the News," which Lardner would inherit. Another of these sportswriters, Charlie Dryden, was called the Mark Twain of baseball, and was an early influence on Lardner's comic and satiric writing. And by this time Ring had already acquired the familiar newspaperman's habit of spending most of the night drinking and talking.

This was the heyday of the famous baseball team, the Chicago White Sox, whose financial corruption in the World Series of 1919 (they lost the series deliberately for a bribe) was a great blow to the popular and provincial young reporter. Lardner was now working as a regular sports reporter on the Chicago *Examiner*, but already in his newspaper articles he was sketching some entrancing portraits of ballplayers, the kind that would make him a celebrated popular writer:

The Sox had a regular infielder named Jack Gibbs, his home was in Brooklyn and his wife's name was Myrtle. He had been graduated from college—*cum laude*—at the age of four, and everybody on the club knew that he could neither read nor write.

When I say that his name was Gibbs, his home was in Brooklyn, and that he was an infielder and his wife's name was Myrtle, I am not telling the truth. But when I say that he could neither read nor write, I don't mean maybe. Give him a sheet of paper with "Jack Gibbs" and "George Washington" written or printed thereon, and he could not tell one from the other. When a new contract needed his signature, he was Madame X.

He suspected that the other players and the veteran scribes were aware of his idiosyncrasy; nevertheless, he persisted in trying to convince them that they were wrong. He would buy a paper and go through it column by column, page by page. He would insist on seeing the bill of fare in hotels or diners, and after a long and careful study, order steak and baked potatoes, or ham and eggs or both.

Well, I don't claim to have brightened many a corner, but I certainly was a godsend to Jack Gibbs. Being new, I could not, he thought, have learned his secret. Therefore, I was the only one in the crowd who could be of real service to him. When we were traveling and he was tired of steak or ham and eggs, he would maneuver to sit with me in the dining car, knowing that I habitually read menus aloud from top to bottom. It was also my custom, he discovered, to turn to the baseball page in a paper and read that aloud just as I did the menu. So he breakfasted with me as often as he could. . . .

Now Lardner's biographer, Donald Elder, is right I think in suggesting that this apocryphally named ballplayer, Jack Gibbs, was one of the sources of Lardner's fabulous Jack Keefe of the Busher letters and *You Know Me Al.*

Meanwhile the young Lardner had moved to the sports page of the Chicago *Tribune,* which was at the time one of the most celebrated newspapers in the country. Among its writers and reporters were such figures as the boxer Jim Corbett, the Pulitzer Prize-winning historian Marquis James, the literary critic Burton Rascoe, the humorist Finley Peter Dunne, the drama critics Percy Hammond and Burns Mantle, the poetry editor Harriet Monroe, and the actress Lillian Russell. Ring Lardner was hitting the big time, and he increased his importunate suit for the hand of the cultivated and wealthy Midwestern girl Ellis Abbott, whom he called "Rabbit" in some early Lardnerian verses:

> What, Rabbitts have come home to roost?
> Is this what you would tell us?
> A full-fledged senior now is she,
> But still heart-whole and fancy free,
> This girl entitled Ellis?

Ellis went to Smith College, in Northampton, Massachusetts, which was very fashionable and advanced for a girl from Goshen, Indiana, and it made Ring somewhat jealous and insecure, as the poem's next stanzas indicate:

Why no, she brought her trunk back home,
Its each and every part,
Then what was it she left behind?
Her fertile brain, her brilliant mind?
No, just her Goshen heart.

Far East of here she left her heart;
Is that what you would tell us?
Ah, rather had she left her shoes,
Her powder rag, the gum she chews
This most forgetful Ellis.

What will she do without her heart?
Why that no one can tell us,
And least of all young Ringlets tall,
Why, no, he cannot tell at all,
So peeved is he and jealous.

We've lived full twenty years and more
And nothing e'er befell us
That stung so much as this same news
That she her Goshen heart did lose;
Is't true? Come, tell us, Ellis.

The "young Ringlets" was indeed very humble and
supplicating and uncertain during the whole period
of his courtship, and the clever Ellis seems to have
done her best to keep him so.

Ring, on tour with the Chicago baseball teams (the
Chicago clubs were his favorite) during their great
period and during perhaps the great period of baseball

itself, always made sure that Ellis knew where he was so that she could write to him, though all too often she didn't.

REQUEST
Right here I'll be until May ten.
A letter I would like ere then;
On May eleventh, home stay's ceased,
I will have started for the east.

R. W. L.

In Cleveland he saw a newspaper headline, "Smith College Senior Fatally Shot After Love Quarrel," and he commented wryly, "The man in the case certainly had a nice way of showing his affection, did he not?" For Ellis's commencement which he could not attend, he wrote some further verse about his sorrow and solitude, and he penned for her an early example of a long and famous series of "Rules":

COMMENCEMENT TIPS
1. Don't commence too young.
2. Don't stay in the east too long after commencing. The west needs you.

Tip number 4 was, "Don't have anything to do with anyone from Amherst." Tip number 5 was, "Don't forget or neglect to send me an account of the proceedings." Tip number 6, "Don't hesitate to call on me if you want any suggestions regarding the proper gowns to wear."

Ending one of his love letters to Ellis in the dialect that he would perfect in his short stories, Lardner wrote: "I hope you'll answer real soon, dear, (you don't mind if I call you dear, do you dear?)." And in January 1910, he journeyed to her parents' large and imposing home in Goshen (they were from the same Midwestern social background as the Lardners, but the Lardners had lost their money, and one son in particular, Ringgold, was associating with very dubious company in sporting and newspaper circles) to ask for her hand.

Now Ellis Abbott was an intelligent, cultivated, and conventional Midwestern girl, quite conscious of her respectable family background and perhaps spoiled by it. Perhaps she had a certain conflict about marrying "beneath her," into the disreputable world of journalists, who in that period were not yet a specialized, college-educated, and conformist group of professional men. Maybe she had been imbued with nineteenth-century notions of being "a lady," of being sought after by young gentlemen, of being a somewhat passive object of adoration on the part of any would-be suitors. In the typical Victorian romance fiction of this period, the heroine was prone to vapors and fainting spells upon the slightest provocation; and the love affair, starting with a look of instant passion, progressed through a series of complicated misunderstandings, physical evasions, and mental blocks to the first pure kiss some five hundred pages later.

Ellis was playing it cool, maybe; in any case she was

a reluctant letter writer even after they became engaged; and Lardner was madly in love, and subject to all the neurotic anxieties of lovers—which he converted into a little comedy of passion. In August of that same year he wrote to her sister Ruby, "You have a peculiar sister entitled Ellis Abbott. I write letters to her occasionally and I don't believe she reads them. At least, she pays no attention to anything in them." He asked to be remembered to the other Abbott sisters, Dorothy, Florence and Jeannette, and signed the letter, "Your affectionate aunt, Ringgold." In another note, addressed to "Rubina C.," he added:

> I want your peculiar sister to be in Chicago on the eleventh day of the coming September. If she is not there on that date and if she doesn't stay more than a week, I will seek death by strangulation and you will be held as accessory before the fact. And please don't think that is meant as a threat. It is merely a friendly warning. I am rather fond of your p.s. [peculiar sister], in fact, I care more for her than I do for my work, or the great game of baseball, or anything to eat.

This early poetry and correspondence about Ring Lardner's courtship is tenderhearted and affectionate and charming—and so sad in view of the later hardships that befell the Lardner family and Ring himself. Ellis and Ring were finally married in 1911. He was still working on the Chicago *Tribune*, but beginning to write for national magazines with large circulations and for newspaper syndicates that paid more for his material. He was already looking east—to New York, the Big Town where the big money was.

Ring and Ellis's first son, John Abbott, was born on May 4, 1912—all four of the Lardner sons were to become well known in their own right, and three of the four die tragic deaths. In 1913 Ring took over "In the Wake of the News," the humorous column in the Chicago *Tribune* that first earned him a more general literary fame. It was a medley of poems, letters, verses from contributors, witty quotations from other writers, epigrams, sports news, and stories and parodies which he began to invent, all in a vein of comedy and satire that anticipated the later and even more literary New York newspaper column of F.P.A., or Franklin P. Adams. Here Lardner used to insert news and gossip of his own family life and children:

TASTE

I can't understand why you pass up the toys
That Santa considered just right for small boys.
I can't understand why you turn up your nose
At dogs, hobby-horses, and treasures like those.
And play a whole hour, sometimes longer than
    that,
With a thing as prosaic as daddy's old hat.

The tables and shelves have been loaded for you
With volumes of pictures—they're pretty ones,
    too—

Of birds, beasts, and fishes, and old Mother
    Goose
Repines in a corner and feels like the deuce,
While you, on the floor, quite contentedly look
At page after page of the telephone book.

In this newspaper column also appeared the first
examples of "the Busher language," which Lardner
brought to national attention, and more of that native
American idiom which he developed in his own work.
See, for example, the miniature baseball thriller called
"The Pennant Pursuit." Its opening chapter reads as
follows (read with care) :

As Verne Dalton strod passed the jymnaseium
one day in April, bound for the college ofice, where
he was going to make arrangmunts for entring the
college next fall, the ball nine composed of 20
(twenty) or more members came out on its way to
the atheletic field. O said Verne I wonder if Ill ever
have a posichion on that team and fight for the glory
of my ama mather, but he did not have much hope
because his parents had said he must devoat all his
time to study.

But Verne Dalton succeeds in becoming the team's
star pitcher, and in Chapter III he looks up into the
stands, filled with "enthustic college men and fair
co-eds," and catches the eye of Lillian Hazelton, daughter of a New York millionaire. And their romance,
doubtful at first, has a happy future in Chapter IV:

That evening at the commencement ball Lillian Hazelton and Verne Dalton became each other's fiancee, but in the midst of Dalton's joy his loved one made a remark that filled him with dispair she said my father will not alow me to wed he whose fortune does not amount to $100,000 (one hundred thousand and no hundreths dollars) Verne Dalton's parrents were poor farmers and he was hopeless when he thought of the amount of money involved. Little did he know that George Hoff the scout for the New York Giants had been hiding behind the stand that afternoon and threw a crack in the boards had watched Verne Dalton's performance. . . .

Now it is true that a long line of humorists had been developing this kind of language. Artemus Ward, Josh Billings, Petroleum V. Nasby, Mark Twain, Finley Peter Dunne ("Mr. Dooley"), among others, had all worked in aspects of the American (versus the English) language. As humorists, they were exempt from the rules of grammar and rhetoric taught in schools and universities, and therefore the public in general did not consider them "good" or "serious writers." (Sportswriters, also, were allowed the same license with language, and they, too, were not considered quite respectable.) Serious writers wrote "proper English," that is to say, they wrote long, involved sentences full of Latinate polysyllabic words, with elaborate clausal construction, and the more adjectives and the more clauses and the more polysyllables they used the better.

Before Lardner's period serious writers never used simple sentences or plain language because that would have been common and vulgar—and literature meant refinement and culture and superiority to the masses. But nobody before Lardner had gone so directly to the people for their language; nobody had listened to folk language so carefully and recorded it so accurately— and even invented it with such precision.

This does not mean that Lardner did not know correct grammar—rather the opposite. To be a great innovator in art you must know all the rules you break. Thus, speaking of the ballplayer Heinie Zimmerman, who was offered one hundred dollars if he would keep his temper, not scream at the umpires, and not get thrown out of the game, Lardner penned one of a long line of Shakespeare parodies:

> The C or not the C, that is the question—
> Whether 'tis nobler for the dough to suffer
> Mistakes and errors of outrageous umpires,
> Or to cut loose against a band of robbers,
> And, by protesting, lose it? To kick—to beef—
> To beef! Perchance to scream—
> Yes, I'll keep still. . . .
> Thus money does make cowards of us all;
> And thus the native Bronix disposition
> Is stifled by a bunch of filthy luc;
> And ravings of my own fantastic sort
> Are all unheard, tho my long silence does
> Disgrace the name of Heinie.

The Lardners now had a second son, James Phillips, born in May 1914. They had also built a house in the Chicago suburb of Riverside with money that Ellis had inherited from her father; but, as he always would, Ring needed money to live on. That is the real origin of the Busher letters, a series of stories he now began writing for *The Saturday Evening Post*, which became his first famous book, *You Know Me Al*, in 1916.

The hero of these letters, Jack Keefe, is a White Sox pitcher who has come up from the bush leagues and is writing to his old hometown friend, Al, about all his new fame and success, his daily triumphs in baseball, in love, in business affairs, and in social intercourse. Of course he is a complete boob who never admits a mistake and appears most confident just when he is on the edge of a new disaster—but how can anything bad happen to a man who has nothing in his mind but himself? The central fact about Jack Keefe is that he has a tremendous bush-league ego which absorbs every experience into his own narrow, ignorant, pompous view of himself. He talks or writes steadily—about himself. He patronizes Al because he has risen so far above him, and because Al is useful to him. Al is, in fact, his only friend, and since Al's side of the correspondence is never given, we are not even sure of that. Al manages Jack Keefe's business affairs back home, but when the Busher changes his mind, he can't understand why his business contracts can't be changed. There is really no sense of objective reality or of truth or of the outside world in him;

he lives in a fantasy world whose single inhabitant is himself. Actually Jack Keefe is really not so different from the rest of us, and while we laugh at him, we had better also take a sharp look at ourselves. Yet by making him so obvious and comic, Lardner also gave his mass audience a chance to make themselves feel superior to themselves.

Jack wins his first game in the "world serious," but even so the sports reporters call him lucky, and he wants to punch their jaws—his favorite answer to any argument. When the players have drinks later on, he waits for them to treat him, and he is always sure he is being overcharged for anything he buys. He is incredibly stingy because he is afraid of being taken for the sucker that he is. He refuses to go to shows or to good restaurants for this reason, and because he is perfectly satisfied anyhow, thinking about himself. He doesn't need outside recreation, and he can't see why his girl friends should either, because he is such a prize to be with. He has two serious girl friends, Violet and Hazel, whom he can't decide between, and he wishes "they was two of me so both them girls could be happy." At the beginning of his big-league career the Busher is fairly successful (although he is never half as good as he thinks he is), and this is what leads him into even more self-indulgence, boasting, vanity, and arrogance. He can't lose; and when he does, he won't admit it; and when he admits it, in spite of himself, he always has not one excuse but several. It is always someone else's fault, and in this respect Jack

Keefe foreshadows another noted Lardner baseball story called "Alibi Ike":

Johnson had fanned four of us when I come up with two out in the third inning and he whiffed me to. I fouled one though that if I had ever got a good hold of I would of knocked out of the park. In the first seven innings we didn't have a hit off of him. They had got five or six lucky ones off of me and I had walked two or three, but I cut loose with all I had when they was men on and they couldn't do nothing with me. The only reason I walked so many was because my fast one was jumping so. Honest Al it was so fast that Evans the umpire couldn't see it half the time and he called a lot of balls that was right over the heart. . . . Well I come up in the eighth with two out and the score was still nothing and nothing. I had whiffed the second time as well as the first but it was account of Evans missing one on me.

The Busher sends a postcard to Violet, who is at the moment out of favor.

I don't care nothing about her but it don't hurt me none to try to cheer her up once in a while. We leave here Thursday night for home and they had ought to be two or three letters there for me from Hazel because I haven't heard from her lately. She must of lost my road addresses.

Hazel hasn't lost his "road addresses," of course; the Busher is finding an excuse for another impending disaster—but whether it is better for Hazel to love him or not to love him is quite another question. What are we talking about? There is no love possible in the Busher's world, because he is incapable of love. To love is to understand, appreciate, and care for another person; and the only person that the Busher appreciates and cares for is the Busher—and strike out the first word, *understand*.

He gets beaten in the next game in "the serious." His arm wasn't feeling good; his fast ball wasn't hopping. "But it was the rotten support I got that beat me. That lucky stiff Zimmerman was the only guy that got a real hit off of me and he must of shut his eyes and throwed his bat because the ball he hit was a foot over his head. . . ." Meanwhile he has had a letter from Hazel—telling him she is married to somebody else—and the Busher says he is "the happyest man in the world." Because now he can marry Violet, his true love all the while: "Now I can make Violet my wife and she's got Hazel beat forty ways. She ain't nowheres near as big as Hazel but she's classier Al and she will make me a good wife. She ain't never asked me for no money." It all seems a dream to the Busher about his love for Hazel: "She was no good and I was sorry the minute I agreed to marry her."

Hazel has married a middle-weight boxer, and she warns the Busher not to come near her or else he will get his jaw busted, but Keefe says there is no danger of that, because he is so glad to get rid of her. He writes that Al and Al's wife, Bertha, will be just as crazy as he is about Violet when they meet her. "Just think Al I will be married inside of a week and to the only girl I ever could of been happy with instead of the woman I never really cared for except as a passing fancy. My happyness would be complete Al if I had not of let that woman steal thirty dollars off of me." But he has neglected to find out if his dream girl Violet is still in love with him, and it turns out that she also is engaged. In preparation for his marriage he has had Al rent a "little yellow house" in Bedford, and now he again needs Al's help to get out of the lease.

It is a common experience, that of creating a complete fantasy life—a girl friend, a romance, a job—which has no relation to reality and which crumbles under actuality. But all of us are not as good as the Busher is in changing his dream life so fast, or rather, in changing the facts and persisting in his dream life. The worse the situation is, the more confidence he has in himself. Lucky man! For within the week he has married a new girl, Florence, whom he is sure Al and Bertha will like even better. But let us not go into the marriage of Jack and Florence in *You Know Me Al*, because it is just too terrible. You can laugh at the Busher at the start of the book, but his disintegration is terrible, and toward the end of the story you begin to ache for him. Florence "creams him"—in every way; she runs his life, takes all his money, and has no use for him. Her cheap relatives sponge on the Busher and leave him when he is flat. Jack and Florence have dreadful arguments constantly, as all Lardner's middle-American characters seem to do when they get married or even when they are just friends or members of the same family. Arguments are the main purpose of conversation and seem to be the only binding factor in human relationships.

When Florence has stripped the Busher of all his money, she leaves him. And he, the stingiest and smartest of men, is driven to desperation by his condition and tries to slip out of his big-league contract. He is fired and returned to the minor leagues; he is finished. If *You Know Me Al* opens on a comic and entertaining note of sporting life in our provincial culture of an earlier day, it also foreshadows the dark and bitter periods of Lardner's later work. If the Busher's universe is run by a kind of hick god, an ignorant deity from the sticks or backwoods, who has singled out Jack Keefe, rather than a useless sparrow, for his special care, this is also a god of vengeance and retribution in Lardner's literary cosmos. Lardner himself came to have a special and deadly hatred for that blind, ruthless, and self-engrossed American individualism which was oblivious of everything and everybody else.

In an older American society, and in traditional European society, too, there were social bonds, such as membership in a class, a clan, a family structure, that kept the individual aware of his relationships with other people. In the Middle Ages, for example, one's social status was fixed and rigid from the cradle to the

grave; a man lived as his father had lived, as his grand-
father had lived, before him. This was also true, as
we've seen, in Lardner's hometown, with its social
structure based on the life of small farmers and
merchants before the advent of the huge metropolitan
centers and their urban and industrial sprawl. But
Ring Lardner's own period, that of the decades before
and after the First World War, saw a great social
change in which all these traditional social bonds were
dissipated and almost disappeared.

Money, success, power—rather than hard work,
character, respectability, and social responsibility—
became the dominant American goals. Money brought
success and power; money bought happiness; money,
it seemed, was everything. Thus the hero of Lardner's
Gullible's Travels, published in 1917, is an extension
of the Busher, and he is already described in more
somber colors. He is a wise boob from the sticks who
is being taken for a ride by a social system he dislikes
but does not understand. He knows he must get ahead
in the world; he must move upwards; he must meet
"better people"—which means richer people—even
though he doesn't know why he has to do this, and he
doesn't like it when he does.

He represents all those ignorant farmboys and small-
town souls of Lardner's period who wanted to get off
the farms and away from the villages and make their
fortunes, become part of high society in the big American cities. This was a new American middle class that
Lardner was describing—without roots, without family

ties, without much feeling for their ancestors, their parents, their history, their home life, their childhood. They were on the go, on the make, rushing to get somewhere else and be somebody more important. These farmboys and small merchants and bush leaguers wanted to get ahead to join the bourgeoisie of the period, and this social movement is reflected in our literature by what Sinclair Lewis called the "Bourjoyces," and H. L. Mencken, the American "booboisie," and Lardner himself entitled "the high polloi." Lardner invented other titles for this new American social class, none of them very flattering, and Mr. Gullible in *Gullible's Travels* is one example of it.

Mrs. Gullible, "the Wife" of Lardner's second important book, is a continuation of the earlier Hazels, Violets, and Florences. Lardner wrote with special spite of the American female of the period, probably because she was taken in by the consumerism of this new American society even more than her usually complaining mate. The wife forces her husband to sell off his stock and take a Florida vacation with her in order to enjoy life and meet some important people and show off her clothes. The first description of the Southern landscape is not exactly enchanting:

Speaking o' the scenery, it certainly was somethin' grand. First we'd pass a few pine trees with fuzz on 'em and then a couple o' acres o' yellow mud. Then they'd be more pine trees and more fuzz and then more yellow mud. And after a w'ile we'd come to some pine trees with fuzz on 'em and then, if we watched close, we'd see some yellow mud.

This is the Lardnerian equivalent of T. S. Eliot's the Waste Land, but the "grand scenery" is a relief compared to the hotel life of the Florida resorts. The Gullibles do meet some "important people" at dinner, but there is no conversation to speak of because all these socially ambitious Lardnerian people are afraid to talk to anybody who may be beneath them on the social-financial scale.

In St. Augustine they spend their time looking at "the oldest house in the United States," eating "the oldest egg in the Western Hemisphere" (according to Mr. G.), riding behind "the oldest horse," and listening to "the oldest jokes." Then comes one of Ring Lardner's typical and incomparable lines: "After supper we said good-by to the night clerk and twenty-two bucks." And when they reach their next destination and Mr. G. sees the bellhops in the hotel grabbing the luggage with one hand and extending the other —palm up—he knows why the place is called Palm Beach. Again he is depressed by the prices and wants to order a room without a bath until the Wife objects. But he is impressed by the building:

Say, you ought to seen that dinin'-room! From one end of it to the other is a toll call, and if a man that was settin' at the table farthest from the kitchen ordered roast lamb he'd get mutton. At that, they was crowded for fair and it kept the head waiters hustlin' to find trough space for one and all. It was round nine o'clock when we put in our modest order for orange juice, oatmeal, liver and bacon, and cakes and coffee, and a quarter to ten or so when our waiter returned from the nearest orange grove with Exhibit A. We amused ourself mean-w'ile by givin' our neighbors the once over and won-derin' which o' them was goin' to pal with us. As far as I could tell from the glances we received, they wasn't no immediate danger of us bein' an-noyed by attentions.

Talk about alienation and isolation as our modern philosophers, particularly the existentialist school, do. Here is a social world of atomized particles, so to speak, whirling and circling around each other, as if in the grip of some blind natural—and social—force, but never touching each other, never even aware of each other, nor wishing to be. During the entire vaca-tion which becomes more and more like a nightmare, the Gullibles neither are spoken to by nor do they speak to anyone except the hotel servants. As if to reinforce this point, *the* Mrs. Potter of Chicago does finally talk to Mrs. Gullible—to ask her to put some towels in Mrs. Potter's room.

And what brilliant repartee is indulged in by those lonesome twosomes whom Ring Lardner described as the average Mr. and Mrs. USA. Perhaps it isn't so much the range of their curiosity and interest that distinguishes their talk as its verbal felicity. At half

past four they go to "the Cocoanut Grove for tea and
dancin'"; they come back to their room to dress for
dinner, and then they eat and "set around till the
evenin' dance starts," when they dance until they are
ready for bed. "'Who do we dance all these dances
with?' I ast her. 'With whoever we get acquainted
with,' she says. 'All right,' says I; but let's be careful.'"
His feet ache even more than hers do; and while
dancing is all right, says Mr. Gullible, you can get
tired of dancing with one partner all night. Yet they
do venture into "the mazes o' the foxy trot. . . . Well,
I guess we must of danced about six dances together
and had that many quarrels before she was ready to go
to bed. And oh, how grand that old hay-pile felt when
I finally bounced into it!"

Well, this is the early Ring Lardner's version of a
typical American couple on an expensive vacation,
having what they call fun; and it is pretty ghastly and
perhaps closer to the average citizen than we'd like to
believe; or do you disagree? Perhaps it seems a little
dated now (in its price scale particularly) or too extreme a characterization of "the booboisie." But what
about the thousands of senior citizens who go to Florida
each winter, and why is it that Ring Lardner's typical
Americans do remind us of senior citizens when they
are still only middle-aged? What does that show about
this writer and/or his society? And about our cultural
values?

If, moreover, Lardner's view of American life was
already morose and sardonic in *Gullible's Travels*

(and of course deliberately exaggerated in both content and expression), this little parable of popular mores ends on a certain note of human warmth and affection. "The Missus" finally concedes her mistake in forcing them to go on such a vacation:

> The mornin' we landed in Chicago it was about eight above and a wind was comin' offen the Lake a mile a minute. But it didn't feaze us.
>
> "Lord!" says the Missus. "Aint it grand to be home!"
>
> "You said somethin'," says I. "But wouldn't it of been grander if we hadn't never left?"

Now what Ring Lardner is saying through Mr. Gullible is that it might have been better if America also had never left its small-town agrarian life in the nineteenth century for the raw, cold, savage, and ugly Midwestern metropolis of Chicago itself. In *The Big Town*, published in 1921, the tensions of contemporary American society are even more extreme, and this "Mr. Gullible" or Mr. USA—the average American of this new money society, money and almost nothing else—is in a worse fix. The book is subtitled "How I and the Mrs. Go to New York to See Life and Get Katie a Husband," and the hero is sandwiched in between *two* terrible specimens of American womanhood—his wife and his sister-in-law. In New York and on Long Island, the women become even more ambitious, grasping, discontented: restless victims of the big money and social pretension.

Mr. USA is living on his deceased stepfather-in-law's "quick returns," his profits on the First World War. But unfortunately this inheritance belongs to his wife and her unmarried sister who are out to travel and thereby move up in the social scale and gain culture in what Lardner termed "the cesspools of society."

In the third episode, "Lady Perkins," the three of them visit a fashionable Long Island hotel because sister Katie

> can't stand the heat. Or the cold, or the medium. Anyway, when it's hot she always says: "I'm simply stifling." And when it's cold: "I'm simply frozen." And when it ain't neither one: "I wished the weather would do one thing another."

There is not much love lost between these Midwestern family members, it seems. And here is Lardner's—or Mr. USA's—first description of this expensive and fancy social resort which replaces the Floridian hotel-factories:

> Was you ever out there? Well, I s'pose it's what you might call a family hotel, and a good many of the guests belongs to the cay-nine family. A few of the couples that can't afford dogs has got children, and you're always tripping over one or the other. They's a dining room for the grown-ups and another for the kids, wile the dogs and their nurses eats in the grillroom à la carte. One part of the joint is bachelor quarters. It's located right next to the dogs' dormitories, and they's a good deal of rivalry

between the dogs and the souses to see who can make the most noise nights. . . .

It is here that we are informed that the urban American middle classes have been forming some new habits in this period of postwar prosperity, which later will be called "the Jazz Age" and "the boom." In the morning, so Mr. USA reports, "the men get up about eight o'clock and go down to New York to Business. They don't never go to work." Around nine o'clock in this sumptuous Long Island hotel resort, which typifies the whole epoch of material prosperity and aimless pleasure-seeking, "the women begins limping downstairs and either goes to call on their dogs or take them for a walk in the front yard." The front yard has a "whole lot of benches strewed round it, but you can't set on them in the daytime because the women or the nurses uses them for a place to read to the dogs or kids, and in the evenings you would have to share them with the waitresses, which you have already had enough of them during the day."

This interesting equality of children and dogs among the moneyed classes in the early 1920s indicates also what was happening to American family life in that period—and to the American woman. Her emancipation from the traditional role of child-bearing and housework and general feminine subjugation was not viewed altogether optimistically by Ring Lardner.

When the women has prepared themselves for the long day's grind with a four-course breakfast, they set round on the front porch and discuss the big questions of the hour, like for instance the last trunk murder or whether an Airedale is more loving than a Golden Bantam. Once in a wile one of them cracks that it looks like they was bound to be a panic pretty soon and a big drop in prices, and so forth. This shows they're broad-minded and are giving a good deal of thought to up-to-date topics. Every so often one of them'll say: "The present situation can't keep up." The hell it can't!

To this early Ring Lardner the fabulous American dream of the twenties already seemed to be an endless nightmare. But what laughter accompanied his indictment! Still speaking of those American ladies of leisure, he added:

By one o'clock their appetites is whetted so keen from brain exercise that they make a bum out of a plate of soup and an order of Long Island duckling, which they figure is caught fresh every day, and they wind up with salad and apple pie à la mode and a stein of coffee. Then they totter up to their rooms to sleep it off before Dear gets home from Business.

And then came Lardner's famous epitaph for the twenties, if you like, uttered as it was just at the decade's opening—or maybe even an epigram about life itself: "Saturday nights everybody puts on their evening clothes like something was going to happen. But it don't."

The Lardnerian fancy, working at top speed here,

lifts itself off the ground of social satire into the realm of beautiful nonsense. Lardner presses his attack on useless wealth and luxury—or what the American sociologist Thorstein Veblen called "conspicuous consumption," consumption for the sake of social prestige, to show off how rich and important you are—by pure ridicule.

> The hotel's got all the modern conveniences like artificial light and a stopper in the bathtubs. They even got a barber and a valet, but you can't get a shave wile he's pressing your clothes, so it's pretty near impossible for a man to look their best at the same time.

In the midst of all this wealth, comfort, and supposed pleasure, Mr. USA takes more and more to drinking and playing solitaire. Again the new American middle class of the 1920s makes a habit of not speaking to strangers, who may be inferior socially. Their individualism makes them highly suspicious of anyone who is not already known to them, which is generally not anyone much; and they couldn't care less about finding out who other people are or what they are like. They are not interested in anything beyond the range of their own narrow personal interests, which makes them very uninteresting. "You'd think," says Ella [Lardner was commemorating in the character of Mrs. USA his own wife Ellis in a friendly and funny way], "that some of these women was titled royalties the way they snap at you when you try and be friends with them." But "titled royalties" don't snap at other people, because they have enough culture and background and personal self-assurance to give them good manners.

The Lardner family itself moved east to Connecticut in the autumn of 1919, and one of their automobile trips with their children from Chicago to Greenwich (Connecticut) must have furnished the material for what became Ring's famous chronicle of childhood, *The Young Immigrunts*, published in 1920. The sketch was intended as a parody of *The Young Visitors*, written by Daisy Ashford when she was a child of nine and introduced to the public by the Scottish writer of whimsy, James M. Barrie; but it gained a life of its own. Lardner wrote it from the viewpoint of his four-year-old son, and Chapter I is entitled "My Parents." "My parents are both married and ½ of them are very good looking" is the opening line.

> The balance is tall and skiny and has a swarty complexion with moles but you hardily ever notice them on account of your gaze being rapped up in his feet which would be funny if brevity wasn't the soul of wit. . . .
>
> I was born in a hospittle in Chicago 4 years ago [so the young immigrunt continues] and liked it very much and had no idear we were going to move till 1 day last summer I heard my mother arsk our nurse did she think she could get along O.K. with myself and 3 brothers John Jimmie and David for

10 days wilst she and my old man went east to look for a costly home.

Well yes said our nurse barshfully.

As we discover, the narrator of *The Young Immigrunts* is Ring, Jr., called Bill, and David, the youngest brother, "is almost nothing" yet in years, and everybody watches him take a bath.

Well my parents went east and dureing their absents myself and brothers razed hell with David on the night shift but when they come back my mother said to the nurse were they good boys.

Fine replid our nurse lamely and where are you going to live.

Connecticut said my mother.

Our nurse forced a tired smile. . . .

Chapter 2, entitled "Starting Gaily," opens with another celebrated line: "We spent the rest of the summer on my granmother in Indiana. . . ."

The two older boys and David travel east on the train with the nurse while the father, mother, and young Bill go by car. The three of them leave Goshen, Indiana, for Detroit, in a series of hilarious episodes, and soon they are steaming upriver on "the city of Detroit 3" on which there is also a newly married couple—"the costly bride and the fare glum."

Oh [says the young immigrunt to himself] I hope they will talk so as I can hear them as I have always wandered what newlyweds talk about on their way to Niagara Falls and soon my wishes was realized.

Some night said the young glum are you warm enough.

I am perfectly comfertible replid the fare bride tho her looks belid her words what time do we arrive in Buffalo.

9 oclock said the lordly glum are you warm enough.

I am perfectly comfertible replid the fare bride what time do we arrive in Buffalo.

9 oclock said the lordly glum I am afrade it is too cold for you out here.

Well maybe it is replid the fare bride and without farther adieu they went in the spacius parlers.

I wander will he be arsking her 8 years from now is she warm enough said my mother with a faint grimace.

The weather may change before then replid my father.

Are you warm enough said my father after a slite pause.

No was my mother's catchy reply.

What Lardner is satirizing here, of course, is described by the title of a recent movie, *Lovers and Other Strangers*. It is not merely the customary awkwardness of two young people on their wedding night. It is the deeper estrangement of two people joined in holy wedlock for the rest of their lives just finding out that they have very little to say to each other. Time may alter this for the better, of course, in terms of common experiences, habits, children, and family life —or it may not. The older couple in this sketch also have little to say to each other, except that the mother wonders if in eight years "the lordly glum" will even care about whether "the fare bride" is warm enough, and the father answers that the weather may change.

Chapter 4 of *The Young Immigrunts* is entitled "Buffalo to Rochester 76.4." They have reached New York State by now, and in another entertaining chapter they encounter a "purring" rainstorm and get soaked in their old-fashioned touring car because the father won't stop to put up the side curtains. (A familiar episode in those days, and family fights have continued since, I imagine, about similar matters.) In Chapter 8, "Hudson to Yonkers 106.5," there is even a moment of parental affection.

I have got a fund of usefull information about every town we come to said my father admireingly for instants this is Harmon where they take off the steem engines and put on the electric bullgines.

My mother looked at him will ill consealed admiration.

And what do you know about this town she arsked as we frisked into Ossining.

Why this is Ossining where they take off the hair and put on the stripes replid my father quick as a flarsh. . . .

He is making a bad joke about the famous prison
in Ossining and the striped prison uniforms. And in
the next town, "where John D. Rockefeller has an
estate," the father makes another bad joke—like so
many other Lardnerian husbands, who feeling domes-
tically imprisoned, seem to resort to this form of verbal
protest. "What is the name of the Rockefeller estate
my mother quired breathlessly." "Socony I suppose
was the sires reply."

In Chapter 9, "The Bureau of Manhattan," the
mother asks the father about their plans to pick up
the rest of the family and reach their home in Greenwich, Connecticut.

> Well then heres the dope uttered my father in a
> vage tone. I am going to drop you at the 125 st
> station where you will only half to wait 2 hours
> and a ½ for the rest of the family as the train from
> the west is do at 350 at 125 st in the meen wile I
> will drive out to Grenitch with Bill and see if the
> house is ready and etc and if the other peaples train
> is on time you can catch the 4 4 and I an Bill will
> meet you at the Grenitch station.
>
> If you have time get a qt of milk for David said
> my mother with a pail look.
>
> What kind of milk arsked my dad.
>
> Oh sour milk my mother screened.
>
> As she was now in a pretty bad temper we will
> leave her to cool off for 2 hours and a ½ in the 125
> st station and end this chapter.

Chapter 10 is called "N.Y. to Grenitch 500.0" and

The lease said about me and my fathers trip from the Bureau of Manhattan to our new home the soonest mended. In some way either I or he got balled up on the grand concorpse and next thing you know we was thretning to swoop down on Pittsfield.

Are you lost daddy I arsked tenderly.

Shut up he explained.

"Shut up he explained" is another famous line from *The Young Immigrunts*; and then, at last, comes the family reunion in "Grenitch."

Did you have a hard trip my father arsked to our nurse shyly.

Why no she replied with a slite stager.

She did too said my mother they all acted like little devils.

Did you get Davids milk she said turning on my father.

Why no does he like milk my father replid with a gastly smirk.

We got lost mudder I said brokenly.

We did not screened my father and accidently cracked me in the shins with a stray foot.

And this is almost the end of what is surely a classic little work in its genre—a genre, however, that is almost purely Lardner's own, and not touched by any other writer I know of except Mark Twain. For what

Lardner and Twain both possess is a kind of unique sense of childhood innocence, of purity of spirit, of a sweetness and happiness of temperament that infuses all the sharp and bitter and usually disappointing outlines of what we call maturity and reality. For life is often an ironic farce of some kind or other, and almost always a tragedy. It is a con game, and you are it. Nobody can go through life without becoming a victim of sorts; nobody can know what the future will bring, except that it is sure to be unexpected, and usually unpleasant. Ring Lardner already knew this himself, but when he wrote about the innocent garden of his children's sheltered life—when he saw his own life through their eyes—his tone was tender and gay; and life itself was a sweet comedy of errors.

This work of Edenic childhood laughter, moreover, marked the end of Ring Lardner's own literary apprenticeship: the early and bright dawning of this talent which was so distinctive, so entertaining, so warm and fresh and touching at its best. We have seen this ourselves in these pages; now what we will see is the maturing of Ring Lardner's work and its tragic end in the process of its hardening and sharpening. The satiric edge becomes keener and razor-thin; the strain of native affection turns harder, more angry, mordant and bitter; the yearning hope of this provincial spirit is blighted by the circumstances around him and the forces within. The Lardnerian pen, in short, becomes almost Swiftian in essence, if it were not for that deep underlying sense of natural humor and beautiful nonsensical playfulness which persisted in Ring Lardner's temperament to the end, and which is perhaps mankind's only defense against the black horrors that can so easily overwhelm our tentative and frail existence.

THE BIG MONEY
2

Ring Lardner himself, just like one of his own characters, came east to the Big Town and the big money in the gaudy postwar era. His writings up to this point are a curious kind of inverted biography in which by identifying himself with the ordinary American boob, he casts a sardonic light on both his own values and aspirations and those of his period.

On the surface, nothing could have been more successful, prosperous, and gratifying than his literary career, his affectionate and entertaining domestic circle. After the Lardners moved to Greenwich in 1919, Ring began to write a syndicated newspaper column that brought him millions of readers.

This column, like "In the Wake of the News" for the Chicago *Tribune*, which it succeeded, consisted mainly of observations about sports and the news in general, personal anecdotes, parodies, little fictional sorties, and whatever appealed at the moment to Lardner's fancy. It was sold to papers across the country by the Bell Syndicate, headed by Lardner's close friend, John Wheeler, who also controlled the works of such other celebrities as the journalist-writer Richard Harding Davis, former President Theodore Roosevelt, the humorist George Ade, the politician William Jennings Bryan, and the evangelist Billy Sunday. What Lardner earned from this column depended on how many papers bought his work; at his peak he reached thirty thousand dollars a year, good money for those times for a sports journalist.

His father, a taciturn and reserved but a very tolerant and understanding and eminently honorable and responsible man, whom Lardner resembled at base even while he inherited his mother's literary and artistic gifts, had died in 1914; his mother, four years later. His last ties with Niles, Michigan, and with the affectionate, leisurely, graceful small-town life of his childhood, were disappearing. Some of his early friends had moved with him from Niles to Chicago, and now his Chicago friends were on the move to New York. New

York was the Big Town, where the money was, where the arts and entertainments were, where the stage and theater were. Among Lardner's newspaper friends, Franklin P. Adams, Percy Hammond, Clare Briggs, and Rube Goldberg, the famous cartoonist, were already in New York, while members of the group known collectively as the Chicago literary renaissance were moving into Greenwich Village, including such figures as Theodore Dreiser, Sherwood Anderson, Ben Hecht, and Floyd Dell.

The Lardners moved with the trend and the times, even though Ring was also moving further away from the earlier American society to which his spirit belonged. The year 1919 marked a revolutionary break with the past in American life: it was almost as though, with a typical time lag, the twentieth century had arrived in one burst of social violence, disruption, and cataclysmic change. Yes, the United States was victorious in the First World War, but the fruits of the victory were almost all bitter. Young writers, those who had served in the army or fought actively or been in the ambulance corps, like Scott Fitzgerald, Ernest Hemingway, John Dos Passos, and the poet E. E. Cummings, experienced a postwar reaction of disappointment, frustration, and anger at American society. And, as Lardner already knew, American society, for all the glamorous flappers and their boyfriends and the drinking and parties—despite the sexual revolution of the period, the easy love, and the easy money—was not an attractive thing. The year 1919 also witnessed

"the Red scare" of the Palmer raids, in which Attorney
General A. Mitchell Palmer prosecuted men and
women suspected of disloyalty to the United States,
political radicals, and anarchists. The real fear was of
the burgeoning Russian revolution; but the real victim
of the scare was the American people, who lost valuable
civil rights in a sort of forerunner to the McCarthy
period of the fifties. In another burst of moral fervor,
equally ludicrous, Congress passed the Volstead Act, for-
bidding the sale of alcoholic beverages, with the result
that drinking increased and flourished on the American
scene as never before, bringing with it the bootlegger
and the beginning of organized crime which threatens
our nation even today. The lurid twenties also witnessed
the arrival of the mass-produced automobile and the advent of necking and petting on a larger scale, thanks to
that more convenient and movable vehicle. The sexual
revolution, celebrated by the short skirts of the flappers, carried along with it the dissolution of the
family—in the Victorian sense of fixed and rigid authority, at least; the automobile brought also a further
mobility—and a greater sense of rootlessness—on the
part of the American population as a whole. And this
emotional, historical, and geographical mobility and
change, which set off this period of "flaming love"—to
use a favorite phrase of the popular literature of the
time—were matched by mobility in the economic and
social spheres. The crooked war profiteers reflected
a general moral laxity in the financial and business
world; in the period of the boom, which lasted all

through the 1920s, the corruption developed to heights unknown before in our history. Everybody wanted a share in the rising stock market, where new fortunes were made every week—or every day. Everybody wanted a piece of the booming real-estate market; whether on Long Island, New York, or in Coral Gables, Florida, for example, fantastic housing developments were often established by selling innocent—and greedy —speculators large plots of land that did not exist or were underwater.

As in Lardner's writings, nobody in this new moneyed society seemed to work very hard anymore; they just went down to the office for a couple of hours, or more usually, they were off on vacations in the south and west of the North American continent. At this time, along with his popular syndicated columns, Ring was also contributing articles and stories to such mass-circulation magazines as *The Saturday Evening Post* and *Collier's*, among others. His work was greatly in demand. (Later on he became "too good," that is to say, too serious for this wide a market; he wrote himself out of it at a great financial loss.) But now he was among the most highly paid of the popular writers. One might estimate that, all in all, he was making around $50,000 a year at his best—or more than $150,000 today—and spending all of it.

From Greenwich the Lardners moved in 1921 to "our heavily mortgaged home in Great Neck," Long Island, which was then a center of literary talent and wealth. His brother Rex, who was never far from Ring, also lived there, and their old friends Arthur and Helen Jacks were neighbors. Franklin P. Adams, the F.P.A. of "The Conning Tower," was another neighbor; Herbert Bayard Swope, the editor of the *World*, another; the sportswriter Grantland Rice was there, too; and so was F. Scott Fitzgerald, the brilliant young star of the post-World War I literary generation, whose *This Side of Paradise*, published in 1920, had created a sensation and set the stage for the Jazz Age. The original flapper of the Jazz Age was Fitzgerald's wife, Zelda, beautiful, talented, and tormented. The stories of their wild parties are legendary, and all of Long Island around Great Neck has been described as one continuous party. It was also the home of that folk hero of the Prohibition period, the bootlegger, whom Fitzgerald immortalized in a later novel, *The Great Gatsby*.

The First World War, then, marked the end of the Victorian period in American culture, and brought in the sexual freedom and social rebellion which some think the hippies invented, but whose historical climax they really embody. From 1922 to 1924 Scott Fitzgerald was Ring's constant companion and drinking partner; it was Fitzgerald who first brought Lardner's writing to the great editor of the period, Maxwell E. Perkins of Scribner's. Ring was fascinated by Zelda's beauty and eccentric talent—"Scott is a novelist and Zelda is a novelty," he wrote—and in turn Ring became a character (Abe North) in what is perhaps Fitzgerald's best novel, *Tender Is the Night*, published

very much later in 1934. It was Fitzgerald who introduced him to the serious writers of his own period;
while in Chicago Ring had not appeared to notice such
figures as Theodore Dreiser and Sherwood Anderson, and oddly enough he did not think Mark
Twain was as great a writer as George Ade or Booth
Tarkington, who were merely popular entertainers.

But Lardner mocked at the glittering, opulent life
of gaiety, parties, and fun in Long Island. While Scott
Fitzgerald was instructing him about literature, Ring
must have had his own private and ironical reflections
about this gifted literary playboy who was so curiously
ignorant about so many other things. Lardner was
wiser and older; he was working too hard and writing
too many newspaper columns and magazine articles to
keep up his standard of living. He was beginning to
sleep badly; he drank too much; and like many newspaper men, he could spend a whole night in talking, in
order to escape from himself.

This is the background of both the humor and the
bitterness of another celebrated sketch written in 1921,
"Symptoms of Being 35," an age at which Ring already
considered himself to be an old man. But the piece is
still funnier than it is bitter.

There is the famous opening line: "The other night
one of my friends whose name is Legion got me on the
telephone some way another and wanted I should come
over and call. . . ." Lardner was a regular poker player,
and his going to "call" had become too expensive, so he
tells his friend he is writing a book for his publisher on
how it feels to be thirty-five.

"That guy must think you got a good memory," says [the friend whose name is] Legion. . . .

Well friends 35 is how young I am no matter how old I look . . . [says the narrator of this chronicle]. When a man has got a legal wife and 4 and no one hundredths children what does he care if he is 35 or double that amt. Besides which they claim that 35 is about average of all the grown ups in the world. If I was above the average would I keep it a secret? Don't be silly.

Here again, in the tradition of all major writers, Lardner was connecting his own singular vision of the world with that of the average man, in this case, the American wise boob. That is to say, he projected the facts of his own life into the mold of the popular thinking of the time, and he also—as is true of all major writers—joined himself to and expressed the general life of his time—as all art is an oscillation of the individual and the general, the general and the individual. In "Symptoms of Being 35," in particular, Lardner casts very personal details—his baldness, for example—in the image of the popular mind:

Personly I am not sensitive about my plummage. When my features got to the decision that one of them would half to retract all I done was thank God they picked the forehead and not the chin. The only hardship connected with pyorrhea of the scalp is trying to act surprised when the barber says you are looseing your hair.

But I guess it ain't only the loss of a few ebony

ringlets that makes me look senile. It seems like I
was over estimated long before I began to molt. . . .

Imperishable and definitive sentences of the Lardnerian language, these are as though written in stone.
Nothing could improve them, and time will not alter
them. These gems of American humorous writing were
almost always written for the popular magazines of
the time. And often, as in another one of these essays
called "Say It With Oil," published in 1923, Lardner
would seize upon and answer—that is, liquidate by
laughter—another article he had read. In this instance,
Nina Wilcox Putnam had written an article on husbands for the *American Magazine* of November 1922.
Mrs. Putnam, a conventional woman's magazine writer
of the time, had uttered the usual trite remarks about
the husband's role in marriage, and this was delicious
stuff for the Lardnerian meat grinder (in this case,
Mrs. Putnam was the ham). Her article was entitled
"Say It with Bricks"; hence the title Lardner used,
but it wasn't oil he was spreading. His words were
poisoned darts that he tossed with hilarious malice in
his defense of husbands, or rather, his description of
wives:

Wives is people that thinks you ought to eat at 8
o'clock, one o'clock, and 7 o'clock. If you express
yourself as having an appetite for turkey at midnight they think you are crazy.

Wives is people that always wants to go home
when you don't and vice versa.

Wives is people that ain't never satisfied as they are always too fat or too thin. Of all the wives I ever talked to I never run acrost one yet that was just right.

Wives is people that thinks 2 ash trays should ought to be plenty for a 12 rm. house.

Wives is people that ask you what time the 12:55 train gets to New York. "At 1:37," you tell them. "How do you know?" they ask. . . .

These observations, he says, are "made without resentment as I have no complaint vs. wives in gen. or anybody's wife in particular. Personly I get along fine with what-ever her name is and I am perfectly satisfied with my home, which I often call my castle. I also refer to it sometimes as jail, but only in a joking way."

That is Ring Lardner on the subject of wives, and you might remember, incidentally, that people who forget names, which is often true of his characters, are people who are so wrapped up in themselves that they have no interest in anyone else. Lardner was approaching his central study of American egotism in a society of prosperity, comfort, and pleasure seeking; but meanwhile he wrote another humorous gem called "Marriage Made Easy." This was in answer to "old Doc Crane's" twenty rules for a happy marriage. (Dr. Frank Crane was a Congregationalist minister of the time who made a fortune writing solemn inspirational newspaper columns and magazine articles.) Lardner explained his own article:

. . . but since the Doc has came acrost with 20 rules on how to be a happy marriage and they are even tougher than the cuckoo test, but it wouldn't make no differents to me as I have all ready got the proposition mastered without no doctor's prescription, but still and all this country is full of young upstarts that may of been just getting ready to assume the connubial yokel and all of a sudden they run acrost the Doc's dope and say it can't be done and they decide to remain celebrates and then what is to become of them 2 grand American institutions, the home and the rent for same.

So in order to perpetrate same by not allowing our young singletons to discourage themselfs with the Doc's dope, I have wrote out a set of 10 simple rules instead of 20 tough ones witch means it won't only take ½ as long to be a happy marriage and twice as easy.

Now these passages are probably among the most brilliant examples of the early Lardnerian dialect, replete as they are with his "young upstarts," "young singletons," "connubial yokels," his young "celebrates," his "2 grand American institutions" which he was perpetrating, and the surrealistic logic of the sentences. But now listen to a few of his simple rules of happy marriage:

The ideal marred life is for the 2 belligerents to live in the same town so as when they feel like a brawl they won't be no toll charges.

If the union is crowned with a offspring, the off-spring should be crowned at intervals by the father. Otherwise the mother should have exclusive rights as care taker as even a baby don't like to change horses in the middle of the night. . . .

As Doc Crane says, it ain't right to find fault with the other on no grounds and the best way is to pertend like you are tickled to death with everything she does. Like for inst. if you are ½ way home on train and she shreaks that she has forgot her pocket book, lean over and give her a good loud kiss.

I could go on and on quoting from these Lardnerian rules for a happy marriage, and I only hope you will get hold of them and read them for yourself, just for fun; but now we are on the brink of his first volume of serious short stories, displaying a different and more complex vein, and a darker side, of this great comic talent.

In the collection called *How to Write Short Stories*, published in 1924—a strange title for a memorable book in our literature—the familiar Lardnerian comedy and parody are subordinated to a more bitter and biting and ironical vision of life.

"The Facts" describes a typical young Chicago businessman who falls in love with the daughter of a typical American family that becomes more and more horrible with each new page of the story. By the grace of God, the hero goes on an alcoholic bender, disgraces himself with each member of the family, and is relieved of his matrimonial obligations—a twist on the conventional love romances of the period.

"Some Like Them Cold" is another Lardnerian dialogue in the form of letters between a man and a girl. Chas. F. Lewis, as he signs himself, has come east to New York to make his fortune as a songwriter on Broadway. The girl is Maybelle Gillespie, whom he encountered in the La Salle Street railroad station just as he was leaving Chicago for "the big town" and to whom he relates the circumstances of his new life. She becomes the "Dear Girlie" of his letters; he becomes the "Dear Mr. Man" of hers. Her letters get longer and longer (and more and more boring); his get shorter as he meets "famous" people in New York and works on his new hit song. The song is called "When They're Like You," and he sends her the chorus:

Some like them hot, some like them cold.
Some like them when they're not too darn old.
Some like them fat, some like them lean.
Some like them only at sweet sixteen. . . .

And so on. The last line of the song is, "But the time I like them is when they're like you" but as he tells her how busy he is and about all the new girl friends he has met, her letters get more uncertain, and he forgets what she has said:

DEAR GIRLIE:
Well girlie have not got your last letter with me so cannot answer what was in it as I have forgotten if

there was anything I was supposed to answer and besides have only a little time to write as I have a date
to go out on a party with the Sears. . . .

She is puzzled by this letter which sounds as if he is
mad at her, and then his next letter, beginning "Dear
Miss Gillespie," tells her that he is engaged. "Betsy is
some doll," he writes, though he adds, "Well girlie I
may write to you again once in a wile as Betsy says she
don't give a damn if I write to all the girls in the world.
. . ." There is only one more letter, Maybelle's answer
addressed to My Dear Mr. Lewis, and the affair is over.

"Alibi Ike" is one of Lardner's most famous baseball stories, because it concerns a star baseball player
who can never admit he is at fault—a familiar type in
Lardner's writings, as we already know from his
Busher stories and as we shall see again later on, and
one not confined to baseball players. Like the Busher,
the Frank X. Farrell of this story is not satisfied with
one alibi if he can find two or three more. He is an out-
fielder who is a good batter, "but he can't hit near as
good as he can apologize"—and by "apologize" Lardner does not mean that Alibi Ike ever thinks of blaming himself. Unlike the Busher, Alibi Ike is really a
great athlete in almost everything he does; only he will
never admit it. He should be even better; there is always something that is hindering him from being as
good as he *really* is.

"He's got the world beat," says Carey [the club
manager]. "I've knew lots o' guys that had an alibi

for every mistake they made; I've heard pitchers
say that the ball slipped when somebody cracked
one off'n 'em; I've heard infielders complain of a
sore arm after heavin' one into the stand, and I've
saw outfielders tooken sick with a dizzy spell when
they've misjudged a fly ball. But this baby can't
even go to bed without apologizin', and I bet he excuses himself to the razor when he gets ready to
shave."

It is a pretty common trait, Alibi Ike's, to always
think you are better than you are. Sometimes a person's imagination is so involved in inventing excuses
that you wonder why human beings go to such ex-
tremes to avoid being honest with themselves. But it
is true, as Lardner so clearly saw, that most of us live
on illusions, not on truth, and particularly on illusions
about ourselves. On the other hand, the truth about
ourselves and our friends is sometimes so cruel, it is
better not to know it.

Nevertheless, "Alibi Ike" is really an entertaining
story, in Lardner's genial vein, with its own sort of
happy ending. This is true of "The Golden Honeymoon," too, another description of Mr. and Mrs. USA
—the typical American wise boob and his sappy mate
—now long married and not very edifying to observe.
The worst of it is that Mr. USA admires his wife.
"You can't get ahead of Mother," he says. In celebra-
tion of their golden wedding anniversary, they are going to Florida, for a winter vacation, and what we soon

realize about this anonymous elderly American male is
that he can't omit one fact—not one single fact—of the
journey. His mind is so empty that he fills it up with
irrelevant data, which he considers essential. He tells
the time their train enters every large city on the trip
south:

. . . We reached Baltimore at 6:30 and Washington, D.C., at 7.25. Our train laid over in Washington
two hours till another train came long to pick us up
and I got out and strolled up the platform and into
the Union Station. When I come back, our train had
been switched on to another track, but I remembered
the name of it, the La Belle, as I had once visited my
aunt out in Oconomowoc, Wisconsin, where there
was a lake of that name, so I had no difficulty in getting located. But Mother had nearly fretted herself
sick for fear I would be left.

"Well," I said, "I would of followed you on the
next train."

"You could of," said Mother, and she pointed out
that she had the money.

"Well," I said, "we are in Washington and I could
of borrowed from the United States Treasury. I
would of pretended I was an Englishman."

Mother caught the point and laughed heartily.

Well, at least the USA's have a sense of humor—but
what *is* the point Mother caught? Still, he is quite a
wit, and she always knows when to laugh. In St. Petersburg—"the Poor Man's Palm Beach"—they spend

their days in the park, watching the horseshoe pitchers and playing checkers and listening to the band. They meet an old friend, Frank M. Hartsell, who is staying in St. Petersburg with his wife, and there is some spirited repartee, dealing mainly with who looks older. The two couples play cards together each evening until the men start competing in the daytime at checkers and horseshoe pitching, and there are harsh words between them. Frank M. Hartsell had been in love with Mother fifty-two years ago, and Father rebukes her:

"I guess he is such a wonderful pitcher and card player that you wished you had married him."

"Well," she said, "at least he ain't a baby to give up pitching because his thumb has got a few scratches."

"And how about you," I said, "making a fool of yourself on that roque court and then pretending your back is lame and you can't play no more!"

"Yes," she said, "but when you hurt your thumb I didn't laugh at you, and why did you laugh at me when I sprained my back?"

"Who could help laughing from laughing!" I said.

"Well," she said, "Frank Hartsell didn't laugh."

"Well," I said, "why didn't you marry him?"

"Well," said Mother, "I almost wished I had!"

"And I wished so, too!" I said.

"'I'll remember that!' said Mother, and that's the last word she said to me for two days.

Now this aging married couple are acting here exactly like children, which is so true of so many marital—

or as Lardner said, "martial"—quarrels, and the worst of it is that either of them could have married someone else without much difference. But they are used to each other, and still have a curious kind of affection in "The Golden Honeymoon," and each pair has a sense of superiority to the other, and this tale of another American couple having another horrible vacation ends on a relatively happy note. And especially so when compared to the famous Lardner story called "Champion."

This is the story of a professional boxer who is a killer and a crook and a liar and who becomes a national hero. It is one of the first of Lardner's really bitter stories, and it signifies his complete disenchantment with "the manly art" as part of the larger American sports scene. Midge Kelly resolves every problem in the world by knocking out his enemies, including women and children and cripples. Heartless and cruel, he has a great sense of humor, too—he thinks. He refuses to spend a cent for the support of his mother, his wife, and his child, while he treats his sweetheart lavishly in order to make a big impression on her. When he gets to the top of his boxing career, he fires his manager for taking too much commission—and promptly has to hire a new one for the same amount because he has no business sense. But his new manager has a wife who is "some doll," as Kelly explains to his sweetheart Grace, and he proceeds to take her away from his new manager. They are all terrified of being hurt or killed by him, with good reason.

When he becomes champion, *The News* does a feature human-interest story on him as an all-American

regular boy, who does not drink, "modest and unas-
sumin' as a school girl," who never talks about himself,
and is afraid of hurting anybody even in the ring,
married, with "four or five" children. The story is read
by millions of people, and the sports editor says there
would have been no point in printing the truth.
"It wouldn't get us anything but abuse to print it. The
people don't want to see him knocked. He's champion."

What Lardner is describing here was a new form of
modern athlete, "professional," ruthless, savage, and
without heart, just as Mark Twain described General
Funston as a new and modern type of American mili-
tary man, one who conquered the Philippines by ruthless guile and mass killings of men, women, and children to "impress" the natives. But at least the millions
of people who do not want to know the truth about
the champion remain good-hearted in their innocence,
ignorance, and need for illusion. This portrait of a
champ is a far cry from the sand-lot baseball of Niles,
Michigan, and the old-fashioned American belief in
sportsmanship and fair play. Perhaps the World Series
of 1919 was still in Lardner's mind, the series when
the Chicago White Sox were bribed by professional
gamblers to throw away the series—and when the actual conspiracy could hardly be believed by baseball
fans and even the hardened sportswriters themselves.
(As a matter of fact, Lardner had broken the news
of this scandal early, in his newspaper stories, and
everybody thought he was just being comic again.)

The specialization, the technical know-how, the industrial-technocratic ethos of a new age, the increasing abstraction and commercialization of society in the twentieth century, had infected and corrupted even the sporting life of the nation: that is also what "Champion" may suggest to us. Among the other literary examples of this in *How to Write Short Stories* is "A Caddy's Diary," the famous story of how people cheat playing golf. And what people! Mr. Thomas is the vice-president of one of the big banks in New York and he always gives Dick, the young narrator of the story, an extra tip.

> Mr. Thomas is one of the kind of players that when it has took him more than 6 shots to get on the green he will turn to you and say how many have I had caddy and then you are supposed to pretend like you was thinking a minute and then say 4, then he will say to the man he is playing with well I did not know if I had shot 4 or 5 but the caddy says it is 4. You see in this way it is not him that is cheating but the caddy but he makes it up to the caddy afterwards with a $1.00 tip.

Dick's best friend is another caddy, Joe Bean, and "to hear Joe tell it pretty near everybody are born crooks, well maybe he is right." Whether Lardner knew his Mark Twain or not, there are echoes of Huck Finn in "A Caddy's Diary," which is also the diary of Dick's education in human morals.

Joe Bean is quite a wit, and the caddies are close students of the wealthy golfers at the club, who hardly ever acknowledge the existence of the boys except when they want to use them as accomplices in their lies. There is a scandal when it is discovered that the club champion, Mr. Crane, who worked in Mr. Thomas's bank and was engaged to Miss Rennie, has stolen eight thousand dollars, and eloped with a pretty stenographer. His fellow members do not understand how he could have ruined "his whole future for $8000"; and then comes the famous ending. Dick and Joe discuss the event, and Dick points out how Mr. Thomas lies for the sake of scoring three less on a single hole, how Mrs. Thomas picks up her golf balls and changes their position to her advantage, and how Mrs. Doane has inveigled him to take her ball out of a rut to help her win her bet.

Well said Joe what of it?

Well I said it seems to me like these people have got a lot of nerve to pan Mr. Crane and call him a sucker for doing what he done, it seems to me like $8000 and a swell dame is a pretty fair reward compared with what some of these other people sells their soul for, and I would like to tell them about it.

Well said Joe go ahead and tell them but maybe they will tell you something right back.

What will they tell me?

Well said Joe they might tell you this, that when Mr. Thomas asks you how many shots he has had and you say 4 when you know he has had 5, why are you selling your soul for a $1.00 tip. And when you

move Mrs. Doanes ball out of a rut and give it a good
lie, what are you selling your soul for? Just a smile.

O keep your mouth shut I said to him.

I am going to said Joe and would advice you to do
the same.

This is wonderful dialogue in the Huck Finn vein of
the early Lardner (and pretty good advice). Is Lardner exaggerating about people and their sportsmanship
in this story? And do you think that sports brings out
the best or the worst side of human nature? I play
tennis with a group of aging suburbanites of both
sexes, and I am convinced that almost everybody cheats
on one occasion or another. It is not that you mean
to cheat or that you consciously do so. It is just that
at crucial points you simply see the tennis ball as being
either out of bounds or in bounds, depending on what
you want to see or need to see. What is interesting in
"A Caddy's Diary" is that these well-to-do golf players
expect the caddies to *assist* them in their cheating, as
though these working-class boys are not human beings
at all, but just another fixture of the country club that
provides such luxurious pleasure and comfort. Money
will take care of it all, or as in Mrs. Doane's case, a
gracious smile will—but the smile is better, all the
same.

The rest of the stories in *How to Write Short Stories*
are in the familiar Lardnerian vein of baseball tales
about dumb, pretentious, utterly self-absorbed athletes
whose talents, remarkable as they are, can never match

their vanity and their own view of themselves. Athletes? Well, they also represent people in general who may not have had the athletes' special skills, or had them in other areas of life.

In his next volume of short stories, *The Love Nest and Other Stories,* published in 1926, Lardner collected his more current stories dealing with Broadway and Hollywood celebrities, songwriters, nurses, and various other characters. Three of these tales—"The Love Nest" itself, "A Day with Conrad Green," and "Rhythm"—are connected stories about show business, an aspect of American life that simultaneously attracted and repelled Lardner; and his stories about this area of American society are among his best and sharpest satires.

The first of them concerns a journalist who is writing up "the great man"—Lou Gregg, president of Modern Pictures, Inc.—and who drives home with him to the great man's magnificent mansion in Ardsley-on-Hudson to meet his beautiful wife (a former motion-picture actress) and his children.

"A wonderful place!" Bartlett exclaimed with a heroic semblance of enthusiasm as the car turned in at an *arc de triomphe* of a gateway and approached a white house that might have been mistaken for the Yale Bowl.

"It ought to be!" said Gregg. "I mean I've spent enough on it. I mean these things cost money. . . .

"But no amount of money is too much to spend on home. I mean it's a good investment if it tends to make your family proud and satisfied with their home. I mean every nickel I've spent here is like so much insurance; it insures me of a happy wife and family. And what more can a man ask!"

And the story proceeds to tell us what kind of a happy wife and family it is that so pleases the great man.

There are affectionate greetings between Lou Gregg and his wife, Celia, who is beautiful and talented and gracious. The children are exhibited briefly before their nurse puts them to bed. The two men drink bourbon before dinner, but Celia doesn't "indulge" because her husband dislikes women who drink. After dinner Gregg is called away to a golf-club meeting, and Celia does indulge, somewhat immoderately.

"Celia poured a whiskey glass two-thirds full and drained it at a gulp. 'It *is* good, isn't it?' she said. . . ." She takes another and another. And she begins to discuss the happy home life—the love nest—of the Greggs as she continues to drink. "The trouble with you, Mr.—now isn't that a scream! I can't think of your name." Bartlett, he tells her, and she calls him Barker. The trouble with Barker, she says, is that he is too sober, and she has to make up for him. And she does. And she adds that she is drunk most of the time. If she wasn't she would die. ". . . Did you fall for all that apple sauce about the happy home and the contented wife? Listen, Barker—I'd give anything in the world to be out of this mess. I'd give anything to never see him again."

But the point is that however obnoxious the movie

magnate is, Celia isn't much better. She has never loved him; she hates him; she married him to get ahead and become a movie star, and he has made her into "a contented mother" who has no use for her children.

"You go back to your magazine tomorrow and write about our love nest. See, Barker?" By this time she is so drunk that Bartlett advises her to go up to her room and get to bed before her husband comes home. When the great man returns, he notices the bourbon bottle is almost empty, and the newspaper man tells him it is delicious stuff. They go to bed after Gregg says they will have a chance to talk together tomorrow on the ride back to the city. "Though I guess you won't have much to ask me. I guess you know all about us. I mean you know all about us now." "Yes, indeed, Mr. Gregg. I've got plenty of material if I can just handle it," Bartlett rejoins.

In the morning Celia, who sleeps late and does not appear for breakfast, calls good-bye to Bartlett and to her husband. "Good-by, sweetheart!" "Good-by, sweetheart!"

Some sweethearts! And in "A Day with Conrad Green"—the title character being another version of Lou Gregg—Lardner gives us a little more detail about the masculine side of these Broadway-Hollywood marriages. We see how the great man functions at work— or rather, as Lardner noticed, in business.

Conrad Green is a producer of Broadway hit shows. He is ignorant, illiterate, stingy, crooked, nasty to his inferiors, and anxious to get ahead socially. He cheats his newspaper boy and the jeweler who has supplied him with expensive pearls for his current girl friend. In fact, he cheats everybody he can and is pleasant only when he has to be. Herman Plant, his faithful secretary and friend—if Green has any friends—has just died, and the producer's schedule for the day has been centered around the funeral. But when Conrad Green learns that his office has already sent forty-five dollars' worth of flowers to Mrs. Plant, he tears up Plant's last paycheck and sends his new secretary to the funeral instead.

Herman Plant is no longer useful to him. Why waste sentiment—and cash? Meanwhile he steals an idea for a comedy sketch from a young writer and relates it to one of his own hack writers as his own idea. But it turns out that the sketch has already been stolen from someone else, and Conrad Green is furious. A scandal-magazine editor next appears and blackmails him into taking an advertisement in his journal because he knows Green has not paid a gambling debt. At the Astor Hotel Green eats a light lunch and tips both the headwaiter and the waiter more than the cost of his meal; it is important to have flunkies who appreciate him. After lunch, his wife arrives unexpectedly at his office and reminds him he has forgotten that it is her birthday. He is forced to give her the pearls he has ordered for his girl friend; and there is another of those inimitable Lardnerian domestic dialogues:

"Oh, dearest!" she cried. "Can you ever forgive me for doubting you?"

She put the pearls to her mouth as if she would eat them.

"But haven't you been terribly extravagant?"

"I don't consider anything too extravagant for you."

"You're the best husband a girl ever had!"

"I'm glad you're pleased," said Green.

Presently his secretary returns from the funeral with the news that Herman Plant had talked about Green's kindness up to the moment of his death; and in the light of the bad day he has just had, Conrad Green says he only wishes he had gone to the service himself. His only reaction to his old friend's death is that he might have escaped some inconvenience if he had not changed his mind about attending the funeral.

The third of these show-business stories, "Rhythm," is less ironical and more openly a comedy of stupidity and immorality. Harry Hart is a popular songwriter who admits he steals his tunes from the great composers of the past and gives them "rhythm"—or a jazzy new twist. When his partner, who writes the lyrics, finally gets worried about this and quits, mainly because his wife believes they will be found out, Harry takes on a new partner who is not so "ravaged by ethics."

The new team turns out another hit show for Conrad Green, and they are "discovered" as native American musical talent by the scholarly critic Spencer Deal. This is Harry's road to fame and prestige—and to his ruin. Overcome by his new glory, he is also overcome by his vanity. He leaves his old friends, his girl friend, his regular haunts and habits, in order to become a serious composer. His own music gets worse and worse; his lack of any personal talent gradually becomes obvious. He ends up broke, and has to start over by returning to his old method of stealing songs from the great composers of the past.

Though Lardner is burlesquing the song-writing talents of Hollywood and Broadway, isn't there also a curious kind of personal element in "Rhythm"? Just reaching toward a different level in his own writing, just emerging in *How to Write Short Stories* and *The Love Nest and Other Stories* from the area of popular journalism, is he also questioning the range and originality of his own literary talent?

Both of these collections of stories have curious prefaces and auctorial notes that suggest this; and, in fact, Lardner never took his own talent seriously enough, even when it was acclaimed by literary critics and intellectuals, like the Spencer Deal whose praise destroyed Harry Hart. Writers like Theodore Dreiser and Ernest Hemingway were also newspapermen in their literary apprenticeship. Before the 1920s many American fiction writers did not go to college. Most of them, like the poet Walt Whitman, were self-educated and usually by their newspaper training; whether the modern generation of college-educated writers will be any better than their predecessors has yet to be proved. There is a question, indeed, as to whether formal education in the United States today tends to produce true originality and character—or streamlines these qualities into social conformity.

The writers I have mentioned were, however, journalists only *on the way* to becoming serious writers; that was always their primary aim. Maybe Ring Lardner had been a journalist too long; maybe he was too burdened by material obligations; maybe he never set his sights high enough and lacked the stubborn faith in himself that artists must have. And maybe, seeing the false egotism, the self-importance, the inflated vanity of the American social types whom he caricatured so brilliantly, he was suspicious of his own ego as an artist. Otherwise, how explain the curious editorial commentary that surrounds the short stories in these first two collections of tales?

In *How to Write Short Stories* (a title suggested by Scott Fitzgerald, but not altogether appropriate for a serious collection of short stories), Lardner introduced "The Facts" as follows:

A sample story of life in the Kentucky mountains. An English girl leaves her husband, an Omaha policeman, but neglects to obtain a divorce. She later meets the man she loves, a garbage inspector from Bordeaux, and goes with him "without benefit of clergy." This story was written on top of a Fifth Avenue bus, and some of the sheets blew away, which may account for the apparent scarcity of interesting situations.

Now this, which is written in Lardner's vein of pure nonsense, is funny, of course, but it is also a strange way to introduce the opening story in a first major collection of short stories. And this vein of personal and literary self-depreciation runs through the introductions to all the stories in the volume. In making his first claim to be a serious writer, rather than a sportswriter or a newspaper and magazine entertainer, Lardner was undercutting his own aspirations and his own talent. Thus he states that the story "Champion" is an example of the mystery story: "The mystery is how it came to be printed." And in his next collection of stories, *The Love Nest*, this strange Lardnerian textual criticism becomes less funny and far more savage and bitter.

The "Preface" to this volume is by "Sarah E. Spooldripper," and Lardner, who had already felt the sad comedy of age in "Symptoms of Being 35," describes himself here, at what was really the threshold of his literary career, as having already been sick and old and dying. If one can argue that this writer was too hard on American life and the people he saw around him, one would have to add that he was hardest of all on himself.

What saved him, indeed, from the utmost depths of despair was the deep vein of humor that he could almost always summon in his writing. We are told that Miss Spooldripper lived with the Lardners for years and took care of their wolf, the wolf at the door, expressing Lardner's constant fear of being unable to support his family's standard of living—one of the worst anxieties a writer can have, and one that the great writers always—well, almost always—try to avoid.

Miss Spooldripper "knew all there was to know about Lardner and her mind was virtually blank. It was part of her charm." (She was modeled on the Lardners' governess, Miss Feldmann, but, of course, she wasn't very much like Miss Feldmann.) "It is hoped that a careful reading of the stories collected in this book," we are told, "will dispel the general illusion that in his later years Ring Lardner was just a tiresome old man induced by financial calamity and a fondness for narcotics to harp constantly on the futility of life on a branch line of the Long Island Railroad. . . ." And if Lardner is satirizing those readers who thought his writing too satirical, there is also an obvious undertone of self-description in such lines. There is more nonsense writing in this Preface to *The Love Nest*, and then a footnote about some imaginary correspondence: "This correspondence and other mash notes written by Lardner and his admirers were obtained from the street cleaners of East Shore Road, Great Neck, where the author threw all his mail . . ."—and, in sober fact, Ring Lardner did destroy most of the correspondence he received, some of it invaluable, and never kept records of his own letters and stories.

"The wolf," Miss Spooldripper writes, "was really the chief interest in Lardner's life." And in the description of the "adoption" of the wolf, there is another one of Lardner's incomparable domestic dialogues:

One afternoon in October while Mrs. Lardner (he always called her Junior as she was two or more years younger than he) was making out the May checks, she suddenly looked up from her work, sobbing, and said:

"Husband!"

"Yes, Junior. What is it?"

"I am overdrawn."

"You stay indoors and brood too much," replied Lardner. "A little exercise and a few pleasures would restore the bloom to both those cheeks."

"I am not referring to anything physical," said the little woman. "I mean there is less than no money in the bank."

At that moment there was a scratching outside that could not have been the children, as they had all had their baths.

"What is that noise, Junior?" inquired the Master.

"I will go and see," said the Madam, sliding head-foremost to the front door, as she was a great admirer of Frankie Frisch.

She returned in a moment, sobbing louder than ever, with the news that the wolf was at the door.

This was the beginning of a friendship that the less said about it the better.

There was "an interesting fact connected with the story 'Zone of Quiet,' Miss Spooldripper adds. "It was written outdoors during the equinoctial gales. Nearly every other sheet of copy was blown away or destroyed

by stray dogs. . . ." Notice how often Lardner stresses
his incomplete, missing, and defective manuscripts, his
letters collected by street cleaners, along with his
wolves and rats and dogs; just as here again he talks
about the early days of "his tepid career." And he describes his own death in this early and brilliant example of what we would today describe as sick humor:

> Those of the tales in this book which have not
> already been mentioned were dashed off after the
> Master had contracted the cold that resulted in the
> fatal attack of conchoid, a disease which is super-
> induced by a rush of seashells to the auricle or outer
> ear. Present during the last hours were only myself
> and the wolf, Junior having chosen this time to get
> a shampoo and wave in preparation for the series of
> dinner dances that were bound to follow. . . .

And now even Lardner's affectionate domestic teas-
ing has a somewhat darker tone, though he reports that
his "Little Nordic" was "quick to take umbrage," and in
fact "Junior was an inveterate umbrage taker and fre-
quently took more than was good for her." And then
there is an almost savage ending to this introduction
to *The Love Nest*. After Lardner's reputed last illness
and death—and we recall Mark Twain's remark that
the reports of his death were greatly exaggerated—
there are some final words: "The Master is gone and
the next question is who will succeed him. Perhaps
some writer still unborn. Perhaps one who will never
be born. That is what I hope." Now Ring Lardner was

not simply being a funnyman here; and he added in the even stronger footnote: "The joke is on Miss Spool-dripper, for she is gone too. Two months ago she was found dead in the garage, her body covered with wolf bites left there by her former ward, who has probably forgotten where he left them."

This is indeed approaching the tone of Jonathan Swift in its savage satire. These curious prefaces to the stories are an ironical and farcical statement of Lardner's true feelings about himself, his career, his work. He wasn't just kidding; rather, their morbid humor allowed him to confess his true state of mind. That "wolf at the door," which represented Lardner's constant fear of not being able to make enough money to maintain his family's standard of living—a standard he himself insisted on for his wife and children—led him to some dark reflections on his own writing career, to wish he had never been born.

Like the introduction, some of the stories in this volume reflect Lardner's increasing despair and frustration about himself. There is less of his charming and delightful play of fancy and lighthearted nonsense. "Haircut," for example, one of Lardner's best-known stories, is told by a small-town barber about a practical joker who is "accidentally" shot to death by the village half-wit. This practical joker has played a cruel hoax upon a young woman who is in love with the village doctor, who is the only person who has been kind to the retarded boy. And what Lardner is really saying is that the half-wit has more sense and more courage than the rest of the townspeople who applauded the cruel jokes of Jim Kendall.

"Zone of Quiet" is another bitter tale, this time about a hospital nurse who entertains her sick patient with a continuous monologue about her own beauty, talent, and sex appeal:

"It seems to me a good many of your cases die." [the patient says to her].

"Isn't it a scream!" says Miss Lyons. "But it's true; that is, it's been true lately. The last five cases I've been on has all died. Of course it's just luck, but the girls have been kidding me about it and calling me a jinx, and when Miss Halsey saw me here the evening of the day you was operated, she said, 'God help him!' That's the night floor nurse's name. But you're going to be mean and live through it and spoil my record, aren't you? I'm just kidding. Of course I want you to get all right."

Does she? She couldn't care less in this story. But he does get better—despite all her "kidding" and the trite and tedious narrative of her own charms and social conquests, which are so transparently false. He is a lucky fellow to escape from this "Zone of Quiet," while his own brief sardonic comments are played off against the nurse's endless and empty chatter. Chatter! Lardner, like the novelist Sinclair Lewis, who wrote at about the same time, could not seem to abide what Lewis termed "the talking woman"; and in "Who Dealt?" another of these gossiping females—who are almost compulsive talkers—holds the floor during a bridge game, or during what should have been a bridge game. Recently married, she unfolds all her newfound marital secrets to her husband's oldest friends while her husband vainly tries to interrupt her complacent confessional—or in plain words, to shut her up:

> I'll stop talking now and try and keep my mind on the game. You needn't look that way, Tommie. I *can* stop talking if I try. It's kind of hard to concentrate though, when you're, well, excited. It's not only meeting you people, but I always get excited traveling. I was just terrible on our honeymoon, but then I guess a honeymoon's enough to make anybody nervous. I'll never forget when we went into the hotel in Chicago——All right, Tommie, I won't. But I can tell about meeting the Bakers.

And she does. After revealing every secret in their married life, reducing her husband to a failure and ex-alcoholic, and after relating a story he has written about the girl he really loved, who left him for a richer, better-educated, more cultivated man (the man to whom she is, in fact, talking), she is astonished to find that Tom's old girl friend Helen has revoked and that Tom has started tossing off drink after drink. The story ends, *"Why, Tom!"* and we never learn what happened after that, but the end cannot have been good. This story is a little gem in Lardner's best vein, and it reminds us again of the talent that is surrounded by such dark omens in *The Love Nest*.

In 1925, the year before that volume appeared,

What of It? was published, another brilliant collection, this time of Lardner's essays and articles. He was at his peak with three such books—*How to Write Short Stories, The Love Nest,* and *What of It?*—all appearing in a cluster in three successive years. But perhaps he knew his best work was past; perhaps he was afraid of the future; and perhaps he felt curiously overwhelmed and bound down by the present. During all the years of popular acclaim, of the drudgery of newspaper work, of always feeling short of money, and of writing too much and too hard to make money, he really was in a trap; the wolf really was scratching at the door. He was walking on sand, as he knew; if his talent should fail him, he would have to walk on water—and already he felt old and sick and worn out long before his time.

THE REALM OF BEAUTIFUL NONSENSE

3

But still, in the contrapuntal melody of his art, in the mixture of oppositions which marked his life and work, the desperation itself produced even wilder and more hilarious moments of fancy; and the sheer need to work, which Lardner despised and which ground him down, produced perhaps some literary creations that a life of plenty and leisure might not have. It was only the artist who had to pay the price.

In *What of It?* were reprinted *The Young Immi-*

grunts and "Symptoms of Being 35" among the other collected essays, sketches, and articles. Perhaps the best new material is the "Bed-Time Stories," in which Lardner translates such classic fairy tales as "Cinderella," "Red Riding Hood," and "Bluebeard" into modern American idiom (in a tradition of our comic literature that runs from Mark Twain's day to the present); and the little surrealistic plays that were originally written for the private entertainment of the actor-members of the Lambs Club, for example, and for the members of various clubs of journalists. Surrealistic or Dada, it hardly matters which term we use to describe them, since they are unique creations.

Dadaism was a French artistic and literary movement that emerged directly after the First World War, not unrelated to the German Expressionist school in painting that developed at about the same time. Both movements were in revolt against the early twentieth-century European society of progress and material comfort and middle-class ("bourgeois") values of property and respectability—a social system that had led to the cataclysm of the First World War itself. In Paris in the 1920s a Rumanian poet named Tristan Tzara was the chief spokesman for a "system of cosmic nonsense" which culminated in bad jokes, obscenities, and violent gestures of protest and disgust. With these literary manifestos, rather like the antics of some of the young American leftists today, the Dadaists sought to show that they completely repudiated the society they lived in—and the art they practiced.

To *épater la bourgeoisie* (to shock and annoy the comfortable, complacent, smug, and rigid middle class) had long been a favorite pursuit of French artists, but the postwar Dadaists carried it to an extreme limit. The First World War had demonstrated the futility of contemporary society, they believed, and their function was to destroy all that expressed this decadent Western European culture. Dadaism was linked to the earlier French Symbolist movement, just as Surrealism to some degree succeeded Dadaism.

Surrealism's most widely known exponent today is perhaps the Spanish-born painter Salvador Dali, who took to using Freudian symbolism to express his despair, and whose most characteristic painting is that of Christ crucified on a mathematical cube— symbolic of the suffering of man today in an abstract society that no longer cares for human values. But Ring Lardner's brand of native nonsense writing was on a relatively simpler, less philosophic, more personal —and funnier—level. In his play "Clemo Uti—'The Water Lilies'" the cast of characters includes Padre, a priest; the twins Sethso and Gethso; Wayshatten, a shepherd's boy; Two Capitalists who "don't appear" in the play; Wama Tammisch, "her daughter"; "Klema, a janitor's third daughter"; and Kevela, "their mother, afterwards their aunt."

Act I takes place on "the outskirts of a Parchesi Board." Acts II and III "were thrown out," Lardner writes, "because nothing seemed to happen." Act IV takes place in "a silo."

Two rats have got there by mistake. One of them seems diseased. The other looks at him. They go out. Both rats come in again and wait for a laugh. They don't get it, and go out. Wama enters from an off-stage barn. She is made up to represent the Homecoming of Casanova. She has a fainting spell. She goes out.

In Act V a couple of salesmen enter who are trying to sell portable houses. The rest of the cast chant, "We don't want Portable Houses," and the salesmen become hysterical. Kevela cries: "What a man!" Wayshatten, the shepherd's boy, asks plaintively, "Why wasn't you out there this morning to help me look after my sheep?" And there is another Lardnerian song:

CHORUS OF ASSISTANT SHEPHERDS
Why did you lay there asleep
When you should of looked after his sheep?
Why did you send telegrams
When you should of looked after his lambs?
Why did you sleep there, so old
When you should of looked after his fold?

Then there is a marvelous passage of nonsense dialogue between Sethso and Gethso, their names obviously showing their twinship, and their imaginary nature. For no reason at all, Sethso cries: "Who is our father?" No reason at all, that is, except that this is one of the oldest and deepest themes in literature and in life alike. In religious terms it is the age-old

cry of troubled and suffering mankind seeking comfort and solace from God the Father. In psychological
terms it is the age-old complaint of troubled children
and uneasy childhood. (Some philosophers have suggested that both these themes are basically the same.)
In literature, the theme has echoed through contemporary writing in particular, starting with the expatriated Irish writer James Joyce, for example, in
his *Portrait of the Artist as a Young Man*. In the case
of Ring Lardner, a writer who was always so close to
the themes of childhood innocence, the line was probably just a natural and unconscious stroke of imagination. Anyhow, when Sethso cries, "Who is our father?"
Gethso replies "What of it? We're twins, ain't we?"
And some philosophers and psychologists might add
that for insecure, aggressive, and warring mankind to
accept this Lardnerian answer is better than search-
ing vainly for supernatural solutions to our dilemmas
or blaming our parents for our own faulty behavior.

But I am surely reading too much into Lardner's inspired nonsense—or am I? It is hard always to be sure
what a writer means. At the play's conclusion, Wama
iterates, "Hush, clemo uti" (*the Water Lilies*) as a
kind of benediction, and "(*Two queels enter, overcome with water lilies. They both make fools of themselves. They don't seem to have any self-control. They
quiver. They want to play the show over again, but it
looks useless.*)" And then comes the final stage direc-
tion: "SHADES." Just as in *The Young Immigrunts*,
what marks off these nonsense or surrealistic or Dada

plays is the essential note of childlike innocence, which is echoed in the last dialogue of Sethso and Gethso. Here Lardner is in his purest and most tender and most humorous vein; perhaps as with all great writers, it was this sense of innocence, of simple pleasure and delight in life, that had been violated most deeply by his later experiences as a sportswriter and journalist; by his studies of professional American athletes, and crooked and framed sports; by his encounters with the cruel, selfish, conceited, and dishonest aspects of show business. The same theme is echoed in his touching and entertaining descriptions of courtship and love, which were afterwards followed by the vitriolic descriptions of typical American married couples and marriage itself. That is to say, it was Lardner's extraordinary sense of innocence about life—and a deep morality—that were violated by the materialistic aspects of American society and of mature life which the rest of us more or less take for granted. It was this deep feeling for the purity of life that led to the bitterness and despair beneath his satire. And this childlike innocence—this sense of Eden and of the Garden of Life and then of the Fall—is precisely what artists retain in their lives, compared with those people who adjust to life, who are realistic or sophisticated or cynical about things. And this is what marks off all great art.

That is why the surrealistic plays, in all their innocence and gaiety and laughter, are such a treasure in Lardner's work, and such a contrast to his increasingly bitter vein of social and human commentary.

Here Lardner's fancy is free of the customary
burdens of commercial writing, and here it roams and
dances most delightfully. In "'I. Gaspiri *(The Upholsterers)*', a drama in three acts adapted from the
Bukovian of Casper Redmonda," the characters in-
clude "Ian Obri, a Blotter salesman"; Johan Wasper,
his wife; Greta, their daughter; and "Ffena, their
daughter, later their wife," in what might have been
an allusion to Richard Wagner's cycle, *The Ring of
the Nibelungen.* There are also "Egso, a Pencil Gus-
ter," and "Tono, a Typical Wastebasket," and "Herbert
Swope, a nonentity." Herbert Swope, as we know,
was the editor of the New York *World* during the
twenties, and one of the Lardners' neighbors in Great
Neck. Ring had developed the outrageous habit of in-
sulting his friends publicly in print; he did this also
with the Grantland Rices; but they seemed to enjoy it,
or else they could not help themselves.

Act I of "I. Gaspiri" takes place on

*a public street in a bathroom. A man named Tup-
per has evidently just taken a bath. A man named
Brindle is now taking a bath. A man named Newburn
comes out of the faucet which has been left running.
He exits through the exhaust. Two strangers to each
other meet on the bath mat.*

FIRST STRANGER: Where was you born?

SECOND STRANGER: Out of wedlock.

FIRST STRANGER: That's a mighty pretty country
around there.

SECOND STRANGER: Are you married?

FIRST STRANGER: I don't know. There's a woman living with me, but I can't place her.

Inspired dialogue in Lardner's domestic vein of writing. Then "a woman's cough is heard offstage left," and "A New Character" asks, "Who is that cough?" "Two Moors" answer, "That is my cousin. She died a little while ago in a haphazard way." A character named "A Greek" adds, "And what a woman she was!" and "the curtain is lowered for seven days to denote the lapse of a week."

Can you really explain the nonsense humor of "I. Gaspiri"? As soon as you try to explain it, it stops being funny. There are all kinds of humor, and very different veins of humor in Ring Lardner's work. And humor has many purposes in literature and in life, as for example, to describe and deflate human pretentiousness and pompousness, self-importance, and hypocrisy. But the vein of Lardnerian nonsense humor has almost no purpose other than entertainment and laughter. It is pure humor, so to speak. It is just plain funny, period. Either you laugh, or you don't. On a more serious level of analysis, you could perhaps say that these plays are the free association of a mind that made marvelously comic leaps from one idea, or even one word, to another; or that here is the humor of disassociation, of removing ideas, objects, people, and words from their usual context, or from the logic and reason which we have come to expect as normal, into an altogether different and unexpected context. Hearing a cough offstage, who would possibly say, "Who is that cough?" Who would expect two Moors to enter the play? Who are the Moors? Where did they come from? Then Lardner suddenly becomes altogether literal, as when the curtain is lowered seven days to denote the lapse of seven days.

"A Close-Up of Domba Splew" is one in a series of imaginary interviews that Lardner wrote as spoofs of, or takeoffs on, the conventional interviews with celebrities of the period:

> Not since the tardy posthumous death of Agera Cholera has the American literati been so baffled toward a rising genius of letters than has been demonstrated in regards to the Italian poet, Domba Splew, who, just a year ago, sprang into world-wide indifference by the publication, in The Bookman, of his verse, "La battia fella inna base tuba" (The weasel fell into the bathtub.)

Here Lardner is destroying literary pretensions as a whole, as well as his own literary production. The opening sentence of this piece—just quoted—is pretty hard to beat, but there are some other good passages.

> The two of us strolled haltingly through his garden, which was an Italian garden with all the Italian dishes in bloom—ravioli, spaghetti, garlic, Aida, and citrous fruits.
> "Is this your diversion?" I asked him.

"Yes," he said toppling over a govvel sprig and breaking his ankle in two places.

"Tell me about your home life," I said with a sneer.

Then there is the sketch called "A Visit to the Garrisons," which, like "Lady Perkins," the episode in *The Big Town* about hotel life on Long Island, anticipates the style of suburban society today:

> For the benefit of folks that is planning or building new homes, or nests as I call them, or have moved into homes all ready built and don't know what to do with all their space, I will try and describe something I seen the other night which it strikes me like it will solve a problem for a big majority of families besides adding to the gen. appearance and comfort of the home (nest).

Now what is striking in this intermediate style of Ring Lardner, illustrated in the passages we have quoted from *What of It?* we should mention here. He had moved away from the broad comic farce of the Busher's language, a deliberately overdone parody of what was really lower-class American speech, into what might be described as middlebrow English, or really middlebrow American. It is really the way you and I talk, isn't it? unless and until we are taught better. It is the way we naturally think, until we learn to use a kind of formal logic to break up this endless streaming of association with grammar or rhetoric,

which are formal—in a sense, false—ways of present-
ing the natural material in the human mind. In the
early twentieth century a group of English writers,
including such figures as Virginia Woolf and the Irish
expatriate James Joyce, had already started to develop
the stream of consciousness into an art form. In a sense
Lardner—with a matchless ear for language, on which
he was also an exacting authority—was "democratiz-
ing" and "Americanizing" this same aesthetic development. In the Busher tales he discovered and perfected
the language of the streets, or of an ignorant and illiterate American social class suddenly thrust into
prominence.

H. L. Mencken, the noted editor and critic of American life in the 1920s, ironically categorized this social
class as "peasants." As we know, Lardner also called
them the "high-polloi" and other such names. But
now the hoi polloi have moved up in the world; they
have more money; they go to expensive and luxurious
Long Island hotels; and they are building their own
suburban homes. As Lardner himself moved up the
social scale, he began to drop the somewhat artificial
and exaggerated language of the Busher, and to
develop, in *How to Write Short Stories,* an even more
subtle—because less mannered—form of American
language. It seems to be natural and artless because
it is, in fact, so brilliantly conceived and so technically
accurate and correct.

It is very easy to develop a Broadway or show-
business style that *seems* to be Lardnerian; but there

is actually only one Ring Lardner and one Lardnerian stylist of his caliber in our literature. He can't be faulted; you can never find an error in this apparently so spontaneous use of common language that he also does such verbal pyrotechnics within such brilliant passages of imaginative fancy.

But what is it that the Lardnerian narrator of "A Visit to the Garrisons" discovered to be such an innovation in suburban housing and life style? It is a *den*—the room which some of you may have been brought up with or in, and which you now take for granted, but which was an absolute novelty in the American home of the mid-twenties.

> This room was a kind of small room next to the living room.
>
> "I don't dast come in here unless I am invited," said Mrs. Garrison. "It is Mr. Garrison's den."
>
> "His what?" I asked her.
>
> "His den," says Mrs. Garrison.
>
> The Mrs. and I was both obliged to laugh at the quaint idear of calling a room a den.
>
> "Mr. Garrison comes in here when he doesn't want to be disturbed," says Mrs. Garrison. "Not even I or Junior dast disturb him."
>
> "Junior!" I says. "Who is Junior?"
>
> "Junior is our son," says Mrs. Garrison. "His real name is Ralph, after his daddy, but we thought if they was two Ralphs in the house, we would get all mixed up. So we call little Ralph Junior."
>
> "A good idear," I could not help from saying.

Both the den and the use of the name Junior are signs of rising affluence and rising social pretension, since after all two Ralphs in this suburban family are a mark of established lineage and ancestry. The den, which was then the exclusive property of Mr. Garrison, has now become the gathering place for the entire family. Often its real function is to save the luxurious living room which is on display only for parties and other social gatherings, and meanwhile remains unused, with darkened shades and plastic covers over the expensive furniture, usually purchased by an equally expensive decorator, in order to impress the friends and neighbors who are brought in for special events.

Now it happens that this modern suburban development in home-making and social intercourse is also reminiscent of that family room of our old-fashioned farming culture which was similarly set aside for special occasions, for birthdays, weddings, anniversaries, and funerals. The modern suburbanites who huddle together after dinner in the family den, while the darkened living room goes unlived in and is really a kind of ghost room, have no memories of their agricultural and peasant backgrounds though, because they have never been related to poor people. They are all rich and rootless, until perhaps next year when they are suddenly bankrupt. But what did Mr. Garrison's den really look like?

Well, the den, as they call it, was furnished with one easy chair, a couch, a straight chair and a desk.

They was two pillows on the couch and one of them red and blue and had the word Pennsylvania worked on it.

"Oh, is your husband a railroad man?" asked my Mrs. who is kind of ignorant.

"You mean the pillow?" says Mrs. Garrison. "No, that's for the University of Pennsylvania, where he attended."

Everybody laughed at my wife's mistake.

But this Lardnerian Mrs., whom everybody laughs at, is recalling an older provincial epoch of American society, from which Ring Lardner himself derived, where to be a railroad man was to be an honorable member of the community.

What the husband of this sketch wants "to describe mostly is the ornaments with which the den was decorated, including a pair of antlers and a mounted tarpon and sailfish.

. . . Other decorations in the room was two shot guns, several pieces of fishing tackle, kodak pictures of the time the Garrisons drove from Chicago to the Coast, a pair of foils, pennants of all the big colleges and last but not least a rather risky picture called September Morn.

"I am always threatening to tear that down and throw it away," says Mrs. Garrison.

"You better not!" says her husband.

"Aren't you terrible!" says Mrs. Garrison.

The laughter was general.

Now I am sure the ornaments in *your* den may be a little more modern than the Garrisons' were. I'd imagine the conversation in your den (if you do happen to live in the suburbs) is a little more grammatical. But is there very much difference between this antique and original Lardnerian den—which contained in it all the elements of the large and sweeping changes in American social life that came about in the 1920s and whose chronicler Lardner uniquely was—and those we see around us today? What we have now is only more of the same; and what most people don't remember is that at that time we entered upon a whole new phase of contemporary American society, one distinguished not merely by suburban wealth but of all that this connoted. I mean such things as the development of the enormous cities themselves, with their wealthy suburbs and their increasingly desperate slums and ghettos, "the Jungle of the Cities" as the German poet Bertolt Brecht called them in an amazingly prophetic play. I mean the development of the American middle class in the 1920s whose special historian Ring Lardner became: that ignorant, self-centered, materialistic "high-polloi" who rose to such quick success and power on the easy money of the twenties, which followed the slippery and often illegal profits of the First World War.

The suburbs were indeed the Lardnerian "cess-pools of society." This was the era of the get-rich-quick philosophy, at any cost, never mind how, which a financial titan like Jay Gould, among others, first proclaimed at the end of the nineteenth century and which actually materialized for the American middle class in the 1920s. The booming stock market, in which so many participated and made fortunes on paper, for a little while, was part of this period also. People were buying everything they could at cut-rate terms or on speculation. It was to prove disastrous in the black days of October 1929, but meanwhile life was gaudy and glorious as the boom market went higher and higher, and people spent more and more money for more and more material comforts and luxuries in what amounted to a mad spree of pleasure-seeking hysteria, a national orgy of materialism. It was a period of national make-believe in which the real world—the world of facts and hard truths and painful experience —was momentarily suspended. As we have seen, this was also the period of Prohibition—of the speakeasies and almost compulsive drinking—of crime and gangsters and brutal killings, a period of greater illegality and more personal and social corruption, morally, financially, politically, than perhaps ever before in our history, while on Broadway and in Hollywood, it was a time of dazzling, spectacular, and lavish musical-comedy extravaganzas.

The Jazz Age it was, indeed, and jazz was perhaps the single best native artistic creation of the period, in which so many American artists became disgusted with their society and went off to live in France, Italy, and Spain, calling themselves variously "the Lost Generation" and the expatriates. As I say, H. L. Mencken,

the leading critic of the period—in which our literature also reached a high peak of creativity—became
increasingly bitter and cynical about this society, and
his *Notes on Democracy*, published in 1926, was one of
the blackest documents ever written about democracy.
Life in the mid-twenties was a far cry from that comfortable, spacious, cultivated, that leisurely, pleasant,
and orderly, provincial society in which Ring Lardner
had grown up in Niles, Michigan. And, no doubt, this
earlier background, far more truly democratic and
native to the history of our republic, but now forever
vanished, was one focal center for his mordant criticism of the new age in which he lived.

THE POPULAR ARTS
4

For if Lardner kept himself curiously apart from the tradition of serious American literature to which his talent entitled him to belong, he was in the very midst of the popular literature and the popular theater of his period. If he was reluctant to discuss high art, he was certainly involved in the big money of the twenties; which in itself, as we've seen, was a period more interested in entertainment than in anything else, which believed that life *was* entertainment.

The years of "normalcy," of Prohibition and the
flapper, were gay, glamorous, exciting, but hardly edifying in either moral or social terms. So different from
his own early background, this period also had a part
in forming his character. Indeed, very often when he
appeared to be satirizing the ordinary American people, "the booboisie," of the period he was also flaying
his own way of life and himself. The Scott Fitzgeralds
were spending over thirty-six thousand dollars a year
in Great Neck and "running a roadhouse," as they
said, before they left for France for both financial
and fashionable reasons. By the mid-twenties most
American writers of the Hemingway-Fitzgerald Lost
Generation had expatriated themselves from a society
they considered gross, materialistic, and empty. It was
only the older members of that literary generation,
men like Lardner, H. L. Mencken, Sherwood Anderson,
and Theodore Dreiser, who condemned their own
society even more severely than the expatriates but
refused to leave it. Yet even if Ring had wanted to
leave, he wouldn't have been able to because his work
was so closely tied to the commercial market of syndicated columns and articles and stories for the popular
press.

His letters written to the Fitzgeralds in 1924 are
among the best personal accounts we have of the period
and of his own group of successful commercial artists.
They are fascinating documents as recorded in Donald
Elder's biography of Lardner, and they are marked by
Ring's comical and touching affection for Zelda, the

first and greatest flapper of them all. (See her own
autobiographical novel, *Save Me the Waltz*.) Thus he
wrote her the following poetic farewell, making fun
of Scott:

> So dearie when your tender heart
> Of all his coarseness tires
> Just cable me and I will start
> Immediately for Hyères.
> To hell with Scott Fitzgerald then!
> To hell with Scott his daughter!
> It's you and I back home again
> To Great Neck where the men are men
> And booze is ¾ water.

Hyères is the town on the French gold coast where
the Fitzgeralds were living, "Scott" is the middle
name of their daughter; but notice the last lines of the
poem, which are truly Lardnerian in that they droop
away, both in meaning and meter, to a sad-funny end.
Or a funny-sad end. With the loyalty and concern
typical of all his friendships, Ring took over the chore
of renting the Fitzgeralds' house, overseeing needed
repairs, and helping Scott out financially from time
to time. But even without the Fitzgeralds, the Fitzgerald life with its round of parties—as described in
Fitzgerald's novels—continued.

"The peace and quiet of Great Neck is a delusion
and a snare, I can assure you," Lardner said in an
interview. "There is a continuous round of parties

in progress here, covering pretty nearly twenty-four hours a day. It is almost impossible to work at times and still more difficult to sleep. Mr. Swope of the *World* lives across the way and he conducts an almost continuous house-party. A number of other neighbors do the same; there are guests in large numbers roaming these woods all the time. Apparently they become confused occasionally and forget at whose house they are really stopping, for they wander in at all hours demanding refreshment and entertainment at the place that happens to be nearest at the moment. The telephone is going almost continuously. Of course wives are useful to answer telephones. . . ."

This atmosphere of Prohibition and parties was hardly conducive to contemplation and creation, and the worst of it was that Ring himself was often among those bewildered and estranged party-goers who stopped at the nearest house for refreshment and entertainment. He slept badly or not at all; he used to spend the nights wandering from one party to another, drinking heavily, sometimes "performing"— singing or talking and improvising a series of "operas" in the vein of his nonsense plays. Here is a sample of a Lardnerian love lyric from one such opera: "Gretchin, I'm retchin' for you." Once when the famous actress Jane Cowl asked him who he was, he replied by asking her what business she was in.

Lardner was friendly with Gene Buck, a songwriter,

playwright, and producer of the period, who lived near Ring in an oversized mansion whose living room Lardner compared with the Yale Bowl. (See the identical comparison used to describe the home of the movie producer in "The Love Nest.") In 1925 Lardner and Gene Buck wrote a musical for the Broadway producer Florenz Ziegfeld which was never produced; Lardner and Fitzgerald had both written sketches for the *Ziegfeld Follies*, those annual musical revues which, starting in Chicago in 1907, combined elaborate theatrical extravaganzas with beautiful naked girls—or, at least, girls as naked as they were allowed to be in that period. Seasoned with "comedy" sketches that were not too far from burlesque, the *Follies* became every year more popular. By the mid-twenties they were a standard feature of the Broadway stage, huge money-makers that would be inconceivably boring to the Broadway audiences of today. (In the thirties the same formula was applied to movie versions of the *Follies*, which became increasingly spectacular and increasingly dull.) Ring was already moving toward the stage and the writing of the musical comedies and operas that he really cared most about; the early musical education he had received from his mother and his own love of music—and his perfect pitch—were all operating here.

In the fall of 1924 the Lardners went abroad. "She whom I married and I are going to leave for France on the Paris, September tenth . . . ," Ring wrote Fitzgerald. "Give my fondest regards to her whom you so generously married." He was playing with his own style now.

Later he again wrote Scott: "I hope you and Thelma or whatever her name is can be ready to go with us to Biarritz for a day or two." The Lardners visited France and England, and Ring did a series of articles for *Liberty* magazine called "The Other Side," which later was published as one of his poorer collections. Lardner was not at ease in his European articles. He seems to have needed to limit himself to his own experiences in American society and even perhaps to only certain sectors of that society—but about these nobody was more observant or wrote better.

He was now at the very center of the high-priced popular entertainment world—or industry; he was apparently at the peak and climax of his career. His letters to the Fitzgeralds are vivid and entertaining documents of the celebrated personages of the time. He wrote that Maxwell Anderson and Laurence Stallings' play *What Price Glory?* "is a bear," that Dorothy Parker's *Close Harmony* "flopped," that the Rube Goldbergs "gave a New Year's Eve party to which 150 people were invited and 500 came. Rube said he never saw so many strangers in his life. Billy Seeman had a lot of the Follies people there to help entertain, but the affair was such a riot that little attention was paid to the entertainment."

During this period, Lardner had been in the hospital having his antrum opened but he was better now, "though if I get up suddenly or stoop over a regular Niagara of blood pours forth from my shapely nostrils." Remember his receding ebony ringlets? If Ring

was not altogether desperate about himself, he had the
most engaging self-mockery, when compared, say, with
the pretentious, pompous virility of an Ernest Hemingway.

On the Fourth of July, 1925, so Ring wrote Fitzgerald, the comedian "Ed Wynn gave a fireworks party
at his new estate in the Grenwolde division":

> After the children had been sent home, everybody
> got pie-eyed and I never enjoyed a night so much.
> All the Great Neck professionals did their stuff, the
> former chorus girls sang, Blanche Ring kissed me
> and sang, etc. The party lasted through the next
> day and wound up next evening at Tom Meighan's,
> where the principal entertainment was provided by
> Lila Lee and another dame who did some very funny
> imitations (really funny) in the moonlight on the
> tennis court. We would ask them to imitate Houdini,
> Leon Errol, or Will Rogers, or Elsie Janis; the imita-
> tions were all the same, consisting of an aesthetic
> dance which ended with an unaesthetic fall onto the
> tennis court.
>
> Charley Chaplin's new picture "The Gold Rush"
> opens here next week and we are going to a party
> in his honor at Nast's.
>
> We do miss you and Zelda a great deal. Write
> again and tell her to write, too. And I might add that
> I have a little money to lend at the proverbial six
> per cent, if worst comes to worst.

The Jazz Age on Long Island was gay and fascinating and brilliant and entertaining (and the parties still

go on today among corresponding groups of fashionable writers). But how much of it could a serious writer take and still continue writing?

Lardner was a "jag writer" (as is common with many newspaper columnists and syndicated magazine writers) as well as a jag drinker. He would write in great spurts at high tension, getting ahead of the deadlines on his columns and articles. Sometimes, when writing a story, he would sit around talking with Ellis until midnight, then enter his study and work all night until the work was finished. And this method was often reflected in the stories themselves, which are technical *tours de force,* with absolutely brilliant aesthetic surfaces, yet without the depth or complexity of a story by Hemingway or Sherwood Anderson or Theodore Dreiser. Indeed, the Dreiserian short stories—heavy, slow, formless, introspective and brooding, reading almost like chapters from a novel—are the very opposite of Lardner's.

By 1926 *How to Write Short Stories* and *The Love Nest* had established Lardner's reputation among the serious critics of the time. Those who early admired his talent included H. L. Mencken; Edmund Wilson; Thomas Boyd, a writer of much promise in those days; and Burton Rascoe, the leading literary critic of the Chicago renaissance.

Maxwell Perkins of Scribner's, the famous editor of the period, had even reissued some of Lardner's earlier books; and Ray Long, the editor of *Cosmopolitan* magazine was paying Ring three thousand dollars for each short story (or the equivalent of ten thousand dollars or more today). "For your next six short stories, $3,000 each, or, for your next twelve short stories, to be delivered at intervals of not more than 45 days, $3,500 each," Long told Lardner. Very profitable and flattering financially, but what kind of a working schedule is that for a writer? No wonder Ring Lardner lived under perpetual tension, that he could not sleep, that he never saw enough of the family and children whom he adored, that he "jag-wrote" and sometimes his stories showed it, and that he drank too much and felt prematurely old and tired. It is a typical pattern among newspapermen and syndicated magazine writers, as I say; it is even an honorable tradition among journalists, who often become alcoholics and die young. And besides, during this period, Lardner discovered that he had contracted tuberculosis. He made himself keep away even more from his family for their sake; he varied between extreme periods of drinking and smoking, which brought him to the edge of acute illness, with periods of enforced abstinence, medical care, and recuperation.

It was typical of his old-fashioned American character that nothing, or at most, very little, of this tension ever appears in his own accounts of his work, his family, or social life; that he refused to discuss the subject and wasted no time in self-pity, even while he continued almost literally to work himself to an early death. This brilliantly comic writer, like many other humorists, lived in a darkness he never mentioned. This great American funnyman is both a tragic and a

completely admirable artist. It almost makes you weep
to think of the pain and sorrow he suffered even while,
to the very end, he kept up that miraculous mood of
gaiety and laughter.

Much of the financial strain, moreover, Lardner
could attribute only to himself. Coming from a family
tradition of wealth and culture, he wanted his own
family to continue in it; and perhaps feeling himself
somewhat of a low-class newspaperman and comedian,
among all these sophisticated Eastern intellectuals, he
wanted—just like his own fictional Hollywood and
Broadway entertainment magnates—to see his family's
way of life shine. At any rate, Miss Feldmann, the
Lardners' nurse (of *The Young Immigrunts*) stayed
on as governess for the boys; and because Ring worried
about his family's safety, he hired a chauffeur, Albert,
who stayed with them for thirty years, and there were
usually two or three other servants. He engaged a
private football coach for his sons, who went to private
schools on Long Island and then to Andover. It was
part of the period to live high—"to burn the candle
at both ends" as the poet Edna St. Vincent Millay said
in her famous verse of the period. But for a serious
writer it was an intolerable burden to carry, and a
stupid one; and in Lardner's case, it was almost a slow
form of suicide which he deliberately chose.

Sometimes he spent his nights in the city, performing at New York's two famous actors' clubs, the Friars
and the Lambs. He dropped in at sessions of the
Thanatopsis Literary and Poker Society at the Algon-

quin Hotel, whose membership included most of the successful popular writers of the period. Here were the columnists Franklin P. Adams and Heywood Broun, the Broadway playwrights and directors Marc Connelly and George S. Kaufman; the journalist and drama critic Alexander Woollcott; and the Broadway composer Paul Lannin, who was a special friend of Ring's. Another close friend was the celebrated sportswriter of that period, Grantland Rice; he and Ring used to go on long vacation trips together, and they built summer homes side by side in East Hampton—a dangerous thing to do with even the best of friends.

During a trip to New Orleans in 1926, there was a famous meeting between Lardner and Sherwood Anderson, which Anderson described:

> There was something loose and free in the little room. How shall I describe it? It was Ring. What we all felt for him was warm affection. I had never known anyone just like him writing in America. He awoke a certain feeling. You wanted him not to be hurt, perhaps to have some freedom he did not have.

Anderson was very perceptive here, and his informal and affectionate account of Lardner makes one realize how stiff and aloof was even the critical praise of Edmund Wilson. (Wilson, with a formalist and classical background in literature, could not get at Lardner's American folk quality, nor his humor.) On the second evening Ring spent in New Orleans, with Anderson, he had been invited to a dull party of wealthy people. After he saw Anderson, he left the party with him immediately, introducing him on the way out "as the author of *The Great Gatsby . . . The Confessions of a Young Man . . . Tess of the D'Urbervilles. . . .*" They stole some of the host's liquor (the host drove his own Rolls-Royce, so that seemed fair) and went off to talk by themselves.

In 1926 Lardner was forty-one years old; he was tired of writing, and perhaps tired of living. His health was dangerously poor, and he decided to give up newspaper work and devote himself entirely to musical comedies and the stage. He had had the deepest attraction for this area of popular entertainment since he first saw the *Follies* in his Chicago years; he had followed the famous figures of vaudeville—now an almost forgotten art; he had worked intermittently in the field in the early twenties, and his experiences, expressed in *The Love Nest* volume of stories, had not been altogether happy ones. Yet he still cherished this vision of fulfillment, and of salvation perhaps, although he was never quite to make it in the one field of the arts he cared about most, and where the tensions would not be so much less as greater. Nonetheless, this is another interesting phase of his career, and the show biz of the twenties and early thirties is very interesting, also, in its own peculiar and exotic way.

We have already noticed his feeling for music and drama, which dated back to the cultural interests of Lardner's mother in the Midwestern scene of his child-

hood. When Ring first went to Chicago, he and his
brother Rex became infatuated with the early Negro
variety shows starring Bert Williams and George
Walker. Ring became a lifelong friend and fan of Williams'—one of the great dancers, singers, and come-
dians of the period—and he collaborated with Williams
on sketches and songs in the later days of the *Ziegfeld
Follies,* when Williams' real talent and originality were
bound down by Broadway commercialism. One of these
Lardner-Williams songs was called "Home Sweet Home
(That's Where the Real War Is)" and goes right back
to Mr. Gullible and the whole strain of domestic satire
in Lardner's work, which, however, was never too
popular on the Broadway stage because it broke too
many theatrical conventions. Most American plays
and musical comedies at that time were incredibly
trite and conformist in plot (consisting of a conventional romance with a happy ending, because the
audience did not want to see real life), in moral senti-
ments about good and evil (no "sin" was allowed, or
any hint of vice, corruption, or aberration in the
human soul), and in writing style as well. Lardner's
native wit, sophistication, his satire on human hypocrisy, were too much for that audience; and he had to
restrain his natural talents. In actual fact, he had much
more personal freedom as a sportswriter, syndicated
columnist, and short-story writer than he was ever to
have writing for the Broadway stage.

Lardner's first real song hit was "Prohibition Blues,"
which he wrote for the popular actress Nora Bayes in

1919 for the show called *Ladies First*. One of his early
songs had the title, "I Wonder What My Stomach
Thinks of Me"—pretty sophisticated humor for the
Broadway audience of the time, which has just about
caught up to Ring Lardner now, over fifty years later.
But for the whole prewar period in general, he had
little luck with his songs, mostly because they were
too original and satirical for a Broadway stage that
was so largely comprised of ham.

In Lardner's early Chicago newspaper days, too, he
met the actor-producer George M. Cohan, who years
later, in 1928, produced a Lardner play about baseball,
Elmer the Great, which Lardner disclaimed in its final
theatrical form, but which was the basis of two subsequent movies, each one a little different from the
other, and both very different from the original story. On
Broadway a writer's script might be completely reversed
by the time of production; a little later on, in Hollywood,
this process of revision was raised to astronomical
heights where often nothing remained of a writer's
original novel but the title—if that, too, was not
changed. And both Broadway and Hollywood directors
and producers were mainly, like Lardner's Conrad
Green, ignorant and illiterate men who were interested
only in what would sell. Considering the fantastic
amount of money that has been invested over the years
in Broadway and Hollywood, the number of good
American plays, or playwrights, is remarkably limited,
and the number of good American movies is almost nil.

So here, too, Ring Lardner was engaged in a field

of popular entertainment that was almost more frustrating and depressing than his work for newspapers and magazines, where indeed he had had a larger audience and was relatively free. Yet his deep compulsion for show business carried him on, and perhaps allowed him to relax a little more in his daily routine. Both George M. Cohan and his partner, the Broadway producer Sam Harris, were good friends of Lardner's in the twenties and encouraged him to write for the stage. He collaborated with Charles Washburn, an old friend and newspaperman, in a comedy turn for the vaudeville team of the period, Gallagher and Shean, whose most famous song starting out "Oh, Mr. Gallagher," "Oh, Mr. Shean," continued with a discussion of the general topics of the day, and ended, "Absolutely, Mr. Gallagher!" "Positively, Mr. Shean!" Does it sound silly to you? A whole generation grew up with this refrain, which is still in our heads as a memory, even while we listen to rock or soul music today.

In the late twenties Lardner found himself not doing too well in what he had dreamed of as a more serious field of writing. (Broadway and Hollywood are bad places for a serious writer, and with the exception of professional American playwrights, like Arthur Miller and Tennessee Williams in our period, those who do succeed there seem always to be aiming at but never quite making the grade elsewhere.) He and his friend Gene Buck wrote a play for the actress Fanny Brice which came to nothing. They collaborated on another play, based on *Gullible's Travels*, which didn't work either; they were continually involved working on plays for Ziegfeld which never succeeded in reaching the stage. For a while, Ring had high hopes for his Americanized version of *Orpheus in the Underworld*, a modernized adaptation of the French composer Offenbach's operetta. This was one of Lardner's more serious ventures, although the original itself is, of course, *opera comique*. It was finally scheduled to be produced by the Actors' Theater, backed by Otto Kahn, the philanthropist and patron of the arts, and directed by the famous Max Reinhardt. But this, too, never came to anything.

Ring was always just reaching something important and always falling just short of it—a familiar story in the entertainment industry. He almost collaborated on a musical with Jerome Kern, one of the top composers of the period and one whom he admired. But they had to guarantee to get the comedian W. C. Fields for the show, and Fields that year—and that tormented genius!—had signed simultaneous contracts with three producers, and would therefore, according to Lardner, be spending the winter either in court or in jail.

One of Lardner's best moments on the Broadway stage, however, came in 1930 with the Ziegfeld production of the musical comedy *Smiles*. (It is from a letter Ring wrote to Fitzgerald discussing this assignment that we learn that Florenz Ziegfeld was the prototype of Conrad Green in "A Day with Conrad Green," which apparently Ziegfeld never read—there are some compensations, it appears, for being illiterate.) Lardner's letter to his son John, then in Paris, described what show business was all about. He was summoned to "help out" in Boston with the lyrics for the costars, or really the three separate stars, of the Ziegfeld show —Marilyn Miller and Fred and Adele Astaire.

While the company was still in rehearsal here in New York, the Astaires threatened to walk out because they didn't have a single song together and demanded two. I wrote them two, to Vincent Youmans' music, for a flat price, and thereby got myself into a world of trouble because one of the two was so very comical that, on opening night in Boston, it stopped the show. This was too much for Marilyn's temperament and she told Ziegfeld she would walk out unless I wrote her a comical one (she being as well equipped to sing a "funny" as Miss Feldmann). Ziegfeld called me up from Boston and asked me to come there and write a song for Marilyn and rewrite three other lyrics that were not so good. I knowing him well, asked for an unheard of advance royalty. . . .

Ziegfeld accepted Lardner's terms, and Ring actually wrote twelve songs for the musical, knowing that only seven of them might be used if the show succeeded at all.

The book of the show, by William Anthony McGuire, was unbelievably terrible as I saw it in Boston. . . .

. . . Paul [Lannin] resigned his job as musical

director at Youmans' suggestion (everybody knew
there was something the matter with the show and
picked on Paul, who was not at fault), but I gather
from latest reports that he is reinstated and that
some of the quarrels have been patched up. The
real trouble is the book and the fact that the three
stars are cutting one another's throats and each trying to help him- or herself instead of the production. For example, the best of my contributions, a
duet and ensemble for the opening of the first act,
will be left out through the protests of Fred Astaire
—the number calls for the presence of some Park
Avenue women in evening dress and he doesn't want
anybody to appear dressed up before his own en-
trance.

The only appropriate comment here is wow! Fred
Astaire was one the great dancing stars of the 1920s
and 1930s whose name is a legend. How childish can
a famous star get? The answer seems to be limitlessly,
according to these Lardnerian memoirs of the Broadway stage in the twenties and early thirties—in one
of its most affluent and successful periods. Later on,
when somebody said the Astaires were trying to steal
the show, Lardner replied it would be petty larceny.
But just before this he had had what was his one big
hit on Broadway, the play called *June Moon*, on which
he and George S. Kaufman collaborated. It was based
on Lardner's story "Some Like Them Cold," but into
the play he poured all his subsequent experience with

Broadway songwriters in general. The show was produced by Sam Harris, and opened in New York on
October 9, 1929, for a very successful run.

But even in this show the Lardnerian script was
popularized; the Lardnerian lyrics were "cute" and
sentimental, rather than really satirical and caustic.
And just after the play opened, on October 29, 1929,
the disastrous crash on the stock market occurred,
where a typical stock like Delaware and Hudson Railroad fell overnight from 224 to 152. This inaugurated
the Great Depression of the 1930s and put an abrupt
end to the boom period, the Jazz Age, the flappers,
and "the dotards," as Lardner said. Gone forever now,
except in the annals of history, was that particular
decade of big money and easy money and crooked
money, of sensational financial and political deals, of
glamorized sports and popular entertainment.

I have already described how these years of so-called
normalcy were, in fact, one of the most abnormal
periods in our history: so bent on pleasure, on profits
at all costs; so shining, glittering, and glamorous on the
surface, so narrow-minded, self-centered, and materialistic underneath; so slippery, dishonest, and corrupt
in every sense—spiritually and morally as well as
socially, financially, and politically. This period has
been glorified in our own day as "the playtime of the
arts," and it witnessed, indeed, the second great flower-
ing of our literature after the heyday of Emerson,
Thoreau, Melville, and Whitman in the nineteenth
century; but it was, in fact, a period full of shame

and scandal and general moral debasement when looked at from a true historical perspective—and its literature reflects this.

Do I exaggerate? Then read *U.S.A.*, the great trilogy of the period by John Dos Passos. Read H. L. Mencken's *Notes on Democracy*. Read Ernest Hemingway's dark stories of despair, and his social commentary on the United States when viewed from the various foreign countries he preferred to live in. The decade of the twenties, which started with such a glow and such a flourish and such promise, ended up not merely financially but spiritually broke.

THE DARK
DEPTHS OF PAIN
5

Even though he was one of the most satiric chroniclers of the period, Ring Lardner's life and career were curiously bound to the twenties, which marked the peak of his fame and its decline. *The Story of a Wonder Man*, published in 1927, was a satirical "autobiography," altogether imaginary, which debunked his own career (and the popular success stories of the period) and again prophesied, as Lardner had done in the introduction to *The Love Nest*, the imminent decease of "the Master." And *Round Up*, the collection of Lardner short stories published in 1929, is one of the essential documents in our literature.

In the last chapter we spoke of Ring Lardner's infatuation with the Broadway stage during the gilded epoch of the twenties—and what was essentially a series of failures, of frustrations and defeats, in that area of his work—playwriting and songwriting—on which he had pinned his highest hopes of fame, success, and the big money. If he wanted to escape the rigors and routines of writing syndicated columns and commercial short stories, he found the new medium even less rewarding, psychologically and financially. The need for money was as strong as ever, only he was exhausted from overwork and too depressed by his frustrations and failures to enjoy his successes. His illness—his tuberculosis and also his drinking—was getting worse, was getting nightmarish; and here we approach the dark and bitter ending of what had been so talented and so financially fortunate a career. Like the French poet Alfred de Musset—of whom it was said that his future lay behind him—Ring Lardner's whole career consisted almost entirely of his early work, with a sudden peak of fame, and a sudden and terrible ending.

Round Up contains all the stories that had originally appeared in *How to Write Short Stories* and *The Love Nest*, plus sixteen others written after the two earlier collections were published. Like Mark Twain, Lardner was always interested in popular and provincial verse

—which such poets as Edgar Guest represented on a higher level—and one of these later stories, "The Maysville Minstrel," concerns a small-town gas-meter reader, Stephen Gale, who writes verse and aspires to be a poet. Like how many thousands of other aspirants, he wants to practice the only art, as Twain observed, for which training is considered unnecessary. (Everybody knows, said Twain, that in order to be a plumber, a carpenter, or a mechanic, you have to have years of training, but everybody thinks he can become a writer with no trouble at all.)

Stephen Gale writes love poetry to his wife:

> Stella you today are twenty-three years old
> And yet your hair is still pure gold.
> Stella they tell me your name in Latin means
>   a star
> And to me that is what you are
> With your eyes and your hair so yellow
> I rate myself a lucky fellow Stella. . . .

This is printed as a jest in a famous New York newspaper column (the equivalent of F.P.A.'s "The Conning Tower") under the title of "The Maysville Minstrel." Like the songwriter Harry Hart who is ruined by taking his talent seriously and going "highbrow" in Lardner's earlier story "Rhythm," Stephen resigns from his job at the gas company and sets to work to be a professional poet. His wife Stella shows him how he can make more money per line for his poetry both by adding lines and by cutting them in half. And then he discovers that the publication of the poem was a hoax, a practical joke, perpetrated by a traveling salesman whom he had considered to be a friend and to whom he had confided his artistic aspirations.

The story is cruel and cutting and etched in acid. Even in its recital of a terrible practical joke, "The Maysville Minstrel" makes you suffer along with the hero in the brief, almost perfectly written chronicle of a provincial put-on.

Wasn't all of life, to this later Lardner, a kind of provincial put-on? We are all dupes in our own way, despite our illusions, our pretenses, and our moments of fame and false glory, and we are all in the end tricked and let down by life in one sorry way or another. Thus the Busher becomes cosmic: we are all bushers and wise boobs. And life will prove it to us.

Lardner must have felt the letdown especially keenly. He had embarked on his career from such a pleasant provincial idyll of Midwestern culture in an earlier and more gracious epoch of history—from a kind of sheltered, innocent, and pastoral life in the comfortable and cultivated small-town society of Niles, Michigan. He had entered upon his newspaper work life with such pleasant illusions about American sports, with such a sharp eye, such a fresh, comic, and talented pen. He had made his way up the ladder with such speed and vitality and comic spirit, and found himself so fast in the big time of Midwestern journalism in its heyday, consorting with such illustrious sportswriters and journalists as those we have mentioned; and then courting successfully such a charming and cultivated young lady as Ellis Abbott with whom he was desperately in love. They had moved ahead in the world so rapidly after the birth of the children whom he always cherished, right into the heart of the Big Town itself, where he associated with even more famous Eastern celebrities, including writers, newspaper editors, actors and actresses of glamorous repute, living in the very heart of that fabulous Long Island society depicted as East Egg and West Egg in Fitzgerald's *The Great Gatsby*. Never mind the bootleggers and other racketeers who sprang up in the age of Prohibition; or the crooked business transactions that became more prevalent; or the oil scandals and land scandals in the period of Warren G. Harding's normalcy. That was all in the swim of things, and the period was swimming along fabulously; it was swinging, wasn't it?

Ring Lardner wanted what his period wanted, only he wanted it more than most, and he got it. He brought such talent to his ambitions, and he worked so desperately hard to make it and to keep it, that he wore himself out physically in the process. He knew deep within him—though how could he tell it to his friends or to his family, his wife and children?—that the glittering game had become a farce and a fraud that was eating up his talent and his temperament and even his wish to live. Still he could only continue the desperate game, though now he was dying from it, and dying also from the drinking bouts he needed in order to sustain his weary spirits, just to keep going.

Nonetheless, another of the late stories in *Round Up* called "Contract" was a masterpiece of suburban satire. It is devastating and hilarious—qualities some critics miss in Lardner's work: the final sense of comedy that overwhelms and disperses the hatred, the laughter of genius, so to speak, which is the only answer to the havoc of life. The Sheltons (like the Lardners, for while Ring's work is never autobiographical and reveals little about his masked and tormented talent, it is always taken directly from what he saw in the life around him, and never purely imaginary, except as all art is a blend of reality and imagination) have just left the city to settle into a comfortable suburban existence. They meet their neighbors, the Frenches, and make a date to go to the Frenches to play contract bridge along with some other neighbors.

> . . . Mrs. Cameron was what is referred to as a statuesque blonde, but until you were used to her you could think of nothing but her nostrils, where she might easily have carried two after dinner mints. Mr. Dittmar appeared to be continuing to enjoy his meal long after it was over. And French had to deal one-handed to be sure his mustache remained loyal.

Can you think of any other writer who—in this squirrel-shooting style—could knock out three characters in three separate sentences?

Then, at this bridge party—in a "surburb," as we've

seen, which for Ring Lardner comprised all of life
—there is Mrs. Dittmar.

> Mrs. Dittmar had married a man much younger
> than herself and was trying to disguise that fact by
> acting much younger than he. An eight-year-old
> child who is kind of backward hardly ever plays
> contract bridge.

And the story continues in this acerbic and comic vein.
Mrs. Shelton who is well aware of her husband's anger
at stupidity, and is expecting him to blow up momentarily, is amazed at his geniality—and fearful. There
is some scintillating dialogue in these pages of "Contract," and the players get worse and worse. They
blame each other, argue over the game, fight with each
other, and in general proclaim their idiocy while Shelton shelters himself—and note how often writers either
consciously or unconsciously select very appropriate or
symbolic names for their characters—in an ominous
calm.

For Shelton is planning his revenge on their bad
taste, their bad grammar, their bad bridge manners—
their general stupidity—and he gets it the next week.
His wife has taken to her bed with a migraine headache.
He goes alone to have dinner with them all (well forti-
fied with liquor) and tells them a few things about
their table manners, their use of grammar, their general style of living. He really does (as we may suspect
Lardner wanted to do, or did); and they throw him
out as "a drunk," and he is very happy—until he finds

the next group of suburban bridge players equally
bad-mannered, and gives up.

This is a nasty and funny Lardner story about the
upper brackets of suburban American society, and one
of his best things. "Dinner" is equally acid and funny,
and very familiar, too, if you have been to formal, or
even ordinary, dinner parties. A young man, Harry
Barton, unmarried and good-looking, is seated at dinner with "two peaches, a Miss Coakley and a Miss
Rell," who are "strikingly pretty." The only trouble
is that Miss Rell will never let him finish a sentence,
and goes into long meaningless monologues while he
waits with his mouth open. Miss Coakley, on the other
hand, is unable to finish a sentence:

> "Mr. Burton, I was just telling Mr. Walters about
> ——I don't know whether you'd be interested or
> not—maybe you don't—but still everybody I've told,
> they think—it's probably——" [Harry says he is
> sure he would like to hear it.] "I hate to bore peo-
> ple with—you know how it is—you'd be too polite
> to—and this is so awfully—well, it isn't a thing
> that—it's just interesting if you happen—people
> in Baltimore—though we've only lived there a
> few——"

Harry decides that if she doesn't complete a sentence in the next two minutes he is going to ask for
another highball. He does, and says he's had a hard
day. And Miss Rell turns on him.

"Oh, are you in the Street? That's what they call Wall Street, isn't it? I should think it would be just thrilling. But I suppose it is hard work, too. You stand there all day and shout at other men, don't you, and they shout back at you? It must ruin your voice. Why, I know we went to the Illinois-Chicago game last fall and I got excited and yelled so for Illinois that I couldn't talk for a week."

"That must have——" [says poor Harry.]

"Do you have football here in the East? . . ."

And she continues for another half page of this brainless monologue until she asks Harry if he plays golf, and he says yes, and she says he ought to try it:

"It's lots of fun, especially for a man." And particularly, she says, for men in Wall Street; and he says, "I'm not in Wall Street"; and she says that now that she has an expert on stocks next to her, she wants to know "what are bulls and what are bears. Father's tried to explain it to me, but I can't get it straight." When she asks him a half page later if he knows anything about bull fights, he says no; and when she asks him if he knows anything about toreadors, he asks, "Who?"

Harry is learning fast, but then he has to take on Miss Coakley for another round, and he asks for another highball, and says he's had a tough day. Here we see the Lardnerian hero immersed in alcohol in order to protect himself not indeed from an evil universe, but from an unbearably stupid and trivial one,

impersonated by these two female goddesses of nit-
witness. Again he says he is not in Wall Street, "not
in any street, not even a path"; but Miss Rell glori-
ously disregards this fact, now that she has made up
her mind he is, and asks him solicitously what college
he graduated from. "The Electoral College," says
Harry, and when she asks him this again, after several
more paragraphs of her thoughts, he answers, "the
War College." She wonders how he can stand shouting
to all those men on the floor of the Stock Exchange,
and Harry says he always carries one of those little
stools that golf fans use in order not to have to stand
so much during a match. After dinner Harry tries to
hide behind the piano, and when Miss Rell finds him
and asks him to play bridge, he says he doesn't know
the game. He tells the hostess that her liquor must be
bad, and he has a headache and has to leave.

"I understand," she says. "You were a darling to
come and I'll never forget it." "Neither will I," he says.

And neither will we. These are brilliant stories in
Round Up, the mature Lardner at his best. On the
subject of hatred in this writer, these tales are just
about as funny as they are angry, and "Dinner" (1928)
again verges on the Lardnerian Dada nonsense. In this
collection also are such familiar stories as "Haircut,"
"Alibi Ike," "Champion," "A Day with Conrad Green,"
and "The Golden Honeymoon," which we have already
discussed. Among the other new stories in *Round Up*
is "Ex Parte," a poorer and rather sadistic tale of a

marriage that was ruined from the outset by the husband's purchase of a brand-new home that the wife,
in her passion for antiques, despises. In desperation,
the husband "antiques" the house with a pair of
shears, a blow torch, and an ax—that is to say, he
destroys it. Every human being, Lardner is suggesting
here, has his tolerance level, and his areas of desperation and insanity. "Then and Now" is another cold
and rather cruel story of what three years can do to a
marriage. Lavishing all his talent and material success
on his own family to an almost suicidal extent, Lardner
can't quite be described as being an advocate of happy
marriages or of the institution of matrimony itself.

"There Are Smiles" is Lardner in a different vein.
This is a sentimental, almost hammy tale of a traffic
policeman and a beautiful and reckless woman driver
—and yet it does move us sentimentally and reminds us
of Lardner's original and basic fund of affection and
pleasure in life. "Anniversary" is the devastating account of one evening in the life of a small-town belle
who has married an incredible bore. He is entirely
content with their life, entirely indifferent to her
feelings; and spends the evenings reading her "ex-
cerpts" from the local newspapers, while she plays
solitaire and cheats. The heroine of this story, hearing
about the exploits of an early friend of hers, married
to a man who goes off on drunken binges and beats
her up, finally begs her husband to give her as an anniversary present, which he has forgotten to bring her,
a sock in the eye—and retires to her bedroom.

This is another of Lardner's fine stories in its texture, and it may remind us of the English novelist D. H. Lawrence's dictum that nothing can equal the unhappiness of a woman who is married to a "good" man. We listen to the dialogue of two people in the closest bond of matrimony who are not merely alienated from each other but, as it were, nonexistent for each other; and the husband's incessant flow of small talk—his moronic monologue—reminds us of the indefatigable Miss Rell of "Dinner." Such highly verbal, if unthinking, characters abound in Lardner's later work, almost as if he were saying that the less a person thinks the more he—or she—talks. And in truth, as we go through life, we often see that people talk in order not to express but to distract themselves.

"Travelogue," another brilliant sketch, concerns two more of these relentless chatterers, male and female, who are competing with each other as to who has traveled the most and best. The story is a parody on psychological emptiness, vanity, and prestige. These Lardnerian figures always think that a change of scene means a change of character, whereas the obverse is true: the more it (the scenery) changes, the more it (the Lardnerian small-town soul, or the human race itself) remains the same. Only, as Lardner would say, more so; travel, this "broadening influence," seems to make the Lardnerian travelers even narrower, more self-centered, and unobservant.

The more one travels, the more one stays at home in this autistic—or entirely self-engrossed, self-ab-

sorbed, not-seeing, not-caring—universe of Ring Lardner's provincial minds. And the accuracy of this perhaps central theme in Lardner's work strikes us more
and more as we grow older.

In *Round Up,* too, is included the story called "My
Roomie," published earlier in *How to Write Short
Stories* but in mood more related to the later group
of tales. This is another grim account of an "eccentric"
ballplayer whose antics outdo anybody else's on the
Lardnerian baseball diamond. He is the wise boob to
outdo all wise boobs. He turns out to be a killer, and
is still altogether confident of himself even when he is
put away in a small-town lunatic asylum. This is one of
Lardner's comic horror tales, and maybe represents his
ultimate vision of deluded and self-deluding humanity.

Another new story, "Nora," summarizes Lardner's
final view of the long-sought-after and enchanted do-
main of show business. It is a sequel to "A Day with
Conrad Green"; bitter, sardonic, ironical, it illustrates
again, and for the last time, how Broadway, Hollywood, and recently the TV studios simply devour
talent, deform and destroy it.

But in the case of Lardner's "Nora," it is false talent
which is falsified by a famous Broadway producer and
his team of hack songwriters. The irony is com-
pounded. The young playwright Hazlett has written
an atrocious and hammy play, that is then seized upon
by the Broadway stage people, completely transformed,
and made more—or less?—atrocious. It is difficult to
say in this never-never land of popular entertainment,

and in this sense Lardner's last word about it is really more genial than not. What happens is horrible nonsense, but it is finally nonsense, and a kind of native (and materialistic) Dada again.

Maybe the most nightmarish version of all of Ring Lardner's "travel stories" is "Sun Cured." Ernie Fretts, the central character, is in the insurance business in Brooklyn. He is still a bachelor, cultivated in his peculiar way, a big spender, a gay dog, who is destroying his health in an effort to retain his youth and have "fun."

> . . . I guess that's the trouble. I mean I got too much time on my hands, and I play around too much. Why, say, it's a wonder I ain't dead, the way I been going. I bet I ain't been to bed before two, three o'clock the last six months. You can't go that pace and not feel it.

It is his secretary who runs the business and who tells him he looks so bad he had better take a vacation in Florida. And he does. Only he meets the same friends and takes part in the same drinking bouts, the same night-long card games in Florida as he did in Brooklyn. He returns home just as exhausted and sick (and just as complacent) as when he went to be "sun cured." On the way home he meets the same man, C. L. Walters, whom he met in the train on the way down, and he tells him the same story of the same identical life of drinks, gambling, and girls.

Ernie Fretts, who is thirty-eight years old, doesn't

indulge in sports because he doesn't want to take any extra chances at his age. "You can't be a youngster all your life," he says sagely—pretentiously, pompously, smugly—even though his own kind of compulsive, frenzied nighttime routine of "entertainment" seems to be pretty rough on a middle-aged bachelor who is still fixed on an adolescent version of "living it up."

The "girls," who have been trying to keep up with him, look like "they'd just stepped out of a wastepipe," Ernie adds, but he feels great.

". . . A trip like this was just what I needed—away from the office a whole month and longer and I ain't even given business a thought.

"That's where so many men make mistakes—not taking a vacation; or if they do take one, they keep in touch with their office all the time and spend the whole trip worrying. . . ."

And he tells us again—since he doesn't remember who we are anyhow, or what he has told us, or anything else except what he thinks is his wonderful way of life—that he has a girl as secretary, or rather a woman of fifty-three, a Miss Clancy, who takes care of his insurance office better than he can, and that she was the one who suggested this vacation. And won't she be surprised to see the change in his appearance when he walks in the office Monday morning, or maybe Monday afternoon (if he spends the first night home drinking and gambling)!

And if "Sun Cured" is Ring Lardner's last word in

fiction upon the panorama of American travel and vacation—on that whole social vista of having "fun" in a society on the make and based almost purely, it would seem, on the pleasure principle—this story is so devastating that it almost compels the reader to say "no comment." What can you say about Ernie Fretts, his business life, and his "social" life? Is it evil? No. Is it immoral? Not really, judged by present-day standards. Does it harm anybody else? No, except possibly the people who willingly join him on this pleasure jaunt by their own choice, and who also think they are living it up. So what is wrong, really? Well, I leave it to you to discover, and to decide. It is the last of the new stories in *Round Up*, and you can read it again and again with increased admiration and almost a sense of awe at its technical perfection; its capacity to say just what its author wanted it to say within just the right aesthetic limits—and that final sense of ambiguousness with which a work of art says to the beholder, "All right, make what you want of me!"

Lardner's tuberculosis, meanwhile, had become worse. He was spending more and more time in the hospital, where much of his last writings were composed. He slept little; yet in the spring of 1931 his letters and some of his articles alike were filled with humor and a kind of touching and despairing gaiety. In Doctors' Hospital, in New York City, he was the center of a talented group of friends who came to see him and entertain him, and he was still able to return for the summer months to the Lardner home in East

Hampton. The children had grown up: John, the old-est son, who was now a reporter on the *Herald Tribune*, and David were living with their parents in an apartment in New York City which they had taken for the winter; Jim was at Harvard; and Ring, Jr., at Andover. But Lardner still had to write popular stories to make the money to support his domestic establishment —and he still did so willingly and at the cost of his own physical health and energy. When he could not sleep at night after one o'clock, he spent the rest of his time writing.

By December of 1931 he was almost not sleeping at all. And many of these nights he spent writing letters to his sons and to his nephew, Richard Tobin, who was then a senior at the University of Michigan and already interested in journalism. Ring was now working for *The New Yorker*, and for that magazine he wrote many of his last satires and his Dada plays. During this period, also, Lardner had begun a friendship with one of the truly great writers of the period, the novelist Theodore Dreiser whose *An American Tragedy* and *Sister Carrie* Lardner admired, although he had certain reservations about Dreiser's style. This was a curious encounter in American letters of one of our most meticulous writers (Lardner) and one of our loosest and most obscure stylists. But this is not to say that Dreiser was not a great writer, far greater than Lardner in the end, because the profound and tragic content of his work makes the question of his style almost a matter of personal opinion. Dreiser's style is simply used against him by those who don't understand his art. Dreiser's *content* triumphs over his style; but style can never make content.

Lardner was writing a sequel to his Busher letters in *The Saturday Evening Post*, which was published as *Lose with a Smile* in 1933. Written for cash, in haste, a superficial return to the style of *You Know Me Al*, this last series of baseball letters, nonetheless, has some good things in it. Sick and dying as he was, there is still a remarkable writer at work here—a far more tragic and bitter writer perhaps, but still an entrancingly funny, wild, and entertaining one. In these last Busher letters about Danny Warner from Centralia, Illinois, there is a parody of the then popular song "My Mom."

> My dad I love him
> My mom she loves him.
> My sister Edna loves my dad.
> He is a wonder
> Will live to be a hundred
> And never made a blunder my dad.
> When I was a lad
> If I act it bad mom would scold me.
> Then I would go to him
> And on his lower limbs he would hold me.
> They's no one greater
> Than my old pater.
> He is my alma mater my pop.

This is Dada-Surrealism—nonsense fantasy in verse —and very sophisticated writing (as you can judge even without knowing the original song) for a story that is really a magazine potboiler; now Lardner could not *prevent* the expression of his native humor, even for commercial reasons. Back at Doctors' Hospital in the spring of 1932, work became even more difficult for him than it had been the previous year, as he wrote to Ellis's sister, Ruby Abbott Hendry, in a letter quoted in Donald Elder's biography:

> . . . There was work to be done, but the mere sight of a typewriter gave me heebie-jeebies. When I was able to subdue them and attempt to work, I was immediately overcome by sleeping sickness, though nothing short of chloroform would put me to sleep in bed. I would lie awake and think of debts and expenses; jump up determined to work; begin to work and either get the shakes or doze off, and then go back to bed and start the whole performance over again. . . .

Tormented words from a writer not given to self-pity and always concealing his own state of mind —and yet directly after this statement Lardner was able to write his famous parody of Cole Porter's popular song "Night and Day." Cole Porter had invented a very snappy refrain to the song, "Night and day under the hide of me/ There's an Oh, such a hungry yearning, burning inside of me." Catchy? And Lardner caught it, with variations first "from Little Ann's pen," as he said, and then by "uncle himself." Here are Little Ann's variants, the second of them in "patois."

Night and day under the rind of me
There's an Oh, such a zeal for spooning, ru'ning
  the mind of me.

Night and day under the peel o' me
There's a hert that will dree if ye think aucht but
  a' weel o' me

And then Uncle composed some variants himself, including:

1. Night and day under the fleece of me
   There's an Oh, such a flaming furneth burneth
     the grease of me.
2. Night and day under the bark of me
   There's an Oh, such a mob of microbes making
     a park of me.

Beautiful? I think so. And the lines are just as fresh and funny as when they were written nearly forty years ago. Notice, too, how well Ring Lardner could use words in writing "serious" or "proper" English (or really, American English), as well as in his vernacular variations. The Cole Porter is still a good song for some of us who grew up on it, and Porter was, of course, a sophisticated and witty lyric writer himself; but the song was immortalized by Lardner. During this period, too, writing as the radio critic for *The New Yorker* magazine (since he could no longer read very much and passed the time listening to the radio), he conducted a curious crusade against "dirty" or "sexy" songs and lyrics, partly justified perhaps, but on the whole, as an earlier Lardner would say, the least said about it the better.

This was now in the depths of the depression years; he was hospitalized and almost unable to write; *The New Yorker* paid very little compared to the popular or slick magazines, and his personal anguish—and some sort of guilt for his previous "loose living" on the part of this almost consecrated family man—did not lessen. And yet there was still the humor. When one of the famous movie actresses of the day, Claudette Colbert, paid him a visit in the hospital, he wrote to Richard Tobin, ". . . I never knew they was so many interns in Doctors Hospital. Every five seconds a new one would come in and say, 'Cant I get you some ice-water, Mr. Lardner?' or 'I'm going out, would you like anything from the drug store?' Her hair is now pink but she's cute, anyway."

But the mass-audience, big-circulation, and big-money magazines were no longer taking Lardner's stories—perhaps he had grown too sophisticated for them. And he sent some to H. L. Mencken's famous debunking magazine, the *American Mercury*, at the same time he was working for the more classy but less well paying—in those days—*New Yorker*. In January 1933 his health had deteriorated so much that he was advised to live in California. From there he still wrote affectionate and charming and gossipy letters to his sons, John, Dave, Jim, and Bill (Ring Lardner, Jr.), and to Richard Tobin. When his feet became enormously swollen from his illness, he ended one of these letters: "Meanwhile, the play's the thing/ Which is worrying the life out of your/ Shoeless Uncle Ring." He was also working on another play with George S. Kaufman, his collaborator on *June Moon.*

This last play, concerning alcoholism and family relationships in marriage (both Ring's, perhaps, and Ellis's), was never finished. In May, Lardner spent a few days in New York. He went about in slippers; his feet were still so swollen. Then he returned to East Hampton for the summer—and for good. He was still interested in the theater, in music, in card playing; but he had few visitors and, according to Donald Elder's biography he was sometimes observed alone, his face in his hands, sobbing. He was exhausted; unable to work, he had been forced to give up the long struggle to support his family through writing; he had lost the wish to be an artist. He was worn down, tired out, without hope, and like any other dying organism, he had lost the will to live. Perhaps the life processes wear down upon us all to the point where death becomes no longer feared but welcome. Perhaps it is the one true gift of life, as Mark Twain said.

The Lardners' old governess, Miss Feldmann—who became famous, or notorious, as Sarah E. Spooldripper who recorded the Master's death in *The Love Nest*— came back and found that now the wolf was indeed at the door. Lardner appeared so sick to her that she insisted upon staying on as his nurse. It was not long.

On September 24, 1933, he was playing bridge in the evening, sitting on a heavily padded chair because he was so thin, and the next morning he had the heart attack from which he never recovered. He was forty-eight years old, and his last illness had lasted for seven, long, weary, and tormented years.

THE LIFE
OF LAUGHTER
6

"The Master is gone," Miss Spooldripper had written, "and the next question is who will succeed him? Perhaps some writer still unborn. Perhaps one who will never be born. That is what I hope." But the joke was on her, because the only writer to succeed the inimitable Ring Lardner was—Ring Lardner. *First and Last*, a big collection of his nonfiction—his essays, short plays, parodies, verse, and articles—edited by Gilbert Seldes, was published posthumously in 1934. And volumes of Lardner's work or books about his work have been published in 1941, 1946, 1956 (Donald Elder's biography), 1962, 1963, and currently, with this present book, in 1972.

And how much is still fresh, lively, entertaining reading in *First and Last*. The long years of suffering, pain, and tragedy are redeemed, as is always the case with a good writer, are redeemed and transcended by the range of Lardner's work published after his death. If a writer has a double soul, as has often been said, he surely has a double life—and the life of his writing, his written work, is really his true and lasting self.

In Mr. Seldes' collection of Lardner's nonfictional work, a sort of companion piece to *Round Up*, appear most of the essays we have discussed from *What of It?*, with some early Lardner material not included in that book, and most of the later work done during his illness. The little essay called "My Own Beauty Secrets" is in the tradition of "Say It with Oil" (on how to be a wife, or wives is people that . . .) and "Symptoms of Being 35." "In a recent issue of a weekly"— Lardner opens in that inimitable vein and wonderful prose style that makes you begin to laugh when you read the first sentence:

> In a recent issue of a weekly a lady star in a English revue, namely Miss Renslaw, who is undoubtedly one of the prettiest ladies that ever just happened, give a interview to a gal which the title of it was a woman's duty to be beautiful plus.

What Miss Renslaw seems to of meant by plus was that you should ought to be smart as well as beautiful. In other words if a gal is just beautiful without no brains why after a wile you get tired of setting around and just looking at her because you think to yourself I could get a copy of the Madonna and set there and look at that. . . .

"A woman [says Miss Renslaw] should give over a few minutes every day to reading something good. Memorize two lines of poetry a day, a paragraph or two of good prose. Add a few words daily to your vocabulary. Do this for no other reason than to keep mentally active, enthusiastic and consequently young."

What Lardner is satirizing here is the popular stereotype of culture as described by "one of the prettiest ladies that ever just happened," one who did not have many brains in her pretty head. What sort of poetry would she find to memorize? And how can you read anything good by spending only "a few minutes every day"? Reading is a habit, which like every habit, takes much time and patience to establish. Those who stop reading after their formal education has ended, as many or most people do, really stop learning and growing, and become static and flat in their personalities. Reading is a form of living, perhaps the best form of living after living itself, or a form of living that gives all its true meaning to the art of living.

If you think that Lardner's satire on Miss Renslaw's

kind of culture is exaggerated, you might listen to some typical suburbanites discussing *their* reading. That is, they skip around mentioning first one and then another of the titles currently on the best-seller list, whether they actually have read the books or not, simply to show how well informed and cultured *they* are. It is a form of literary gamesmanship that is imperative in cultivated middle-class circles in American society, but it is not the kind of reading I intended to describe above.

There is another entertaining little essay on dogs in *First and Last,* in which Lardner refutes the fact that if you are kind to animals you can't be all bad. You can be, he says, and proves it.

But as long as our best people has got it in their skull that a friendly feeling toward dumb brutes takes the curse off a bad egg, why I or nobody else is going to be a sucker enough to come out and admit that all the horses, rams and oxen in the world could drop dead tomorrow morning without us batting an eye.

Ring Lardner on dogs then goes on to describe all the screens in the Lardner house which their present dog has broken, "and all the bugs that didn't already live in the house is moveing in and bringing their family." He concluded that he was crazy about dogs in their place, but their place was not Long Island. And he was hardly less caustic about horses:

A horse is the most overestimated animal in the world with the possible exception of a police dog. For every incidence where a horse has saved a human life I can dig you up a 100 incidents where they have killed people by falling off them or trampling them down or both. Personly, the only horse who I ever set on their back throwed me off on my bosom before I had road him 20 ft. and did the horse wait to see if I was hurt, no.

What prose sentences are in here, and perhaps this is the real Lardnerian style at its best, his middle-American style that caught all the nuances and subtleties of the common oral language and refined it into hard lasting prose. It is a style that avoids the excesses and mannerisms of his tales in dialect, but is yet richer, funnier, and altogether more lovely than the straight prose style of his serious stories—a style, finally, that has something of the wistful innocence of "The Young Immigrunts" in it, while it mocks at the fads and fashions of popular culture; and something of Lardner's own central vein of tenderness, even when it is most savage in its satire.

Devotees of horse flesh [he continues] is wont to point out that King Richard III once offered his kingdom for one of them, but in the first place he was not the kind of a person who I would pin any faith on his judgment of values and the second place the kingdom had been acquired by a couple of mild little murders and it was a case of easy come, easy go.

This is standard Lardner prose, in his mature and late work; and it is a lovely style, as I say, to brood upon (it is almost impossible to "analyze" it, but try if you can), and to listen to, or simply to copy down and look for its little turns and tricks. It is in fact almost an impossible style to copy, and you have to watch it very closely to get it right.

One essay in *First and Last* on "How Winners Quit Winners," gives some rules (Lardner's rules!) on how to quit a poker game when you are ahead. Another essay, on "Salt Water Fishing," is pure Dada again.

> The lap-eared smike runs in schools off the coast of eastern Pittsburgh and is caught with live bait like a horse or a canteloupe. Use a No. 12 hook and a E string.

Two other articles, "The Origin of Football" and "New Golf Accessories," are less funny. Even Lardner's vein of humor was running dry; but the miracle is, of course, how he kept writing as many good things as he did during the last years of sickness and sorrow. Covering the famous international America's Cup races in 1930 between Sir Thomas Lipton's *Shamrock* and the American yacht *Resolute*, Lardner was positively morbid. He hated yacht races in general, and he hated this yacht race in particular. He spent most of the time below deck on the destroyer that had been assigned to the newspapermen and sportswriters.

> As I couldn't stand the excitement of continuously watching the 2 catboats as they sped forwards

in the teeth of a 3 mile carm, I happened to be down in Lieut. Annotoyn's room when the Resolute done a Willard [was knocked out]. . . .

Lardner is always going "out on the porch" (the deck) to ask the other sportswriters what happened, and what they tell him about the race never means much to him.

So I borrowed a pair of opera glasses off of a bum cartoonist and took a look at the Irresolute and it looked to me like she had croaked from a barnacle on her binnacle. . . .

Yet even here, in what started out to be a diatribe about the international yacht races, there were moments of brilliant satire. This was indeed a comic reversal on Hemingway's by now notorious concept of *nada,* or nothingness. For Lardner, the saving gift of laughter was man's contribution to the tragedy or the debacle.

Also included in this posthumous collection of Ring Lardner's nonfiction is the famous account "A World's Serious," which centered around his wife's new fur coat:

Maybe I would better exclaim myself before going any further. Well, a few days previous to the serious of 1919 I was approached by a young lady who I soon recognized as my wife, and any way this woman says would I buy her a fur coat as the winter was comeing on and we was going to spend it in Connecticut which is not genally considered one of the tropics.

"But don't do it," she says, "unless you have got the money to spare because of course I can get along without it. In fact," she added bursting into teers, "I am so used to getting along without this, that and the other thing that maybe it would be best for you not to buy me that coat after all as the sight of a luxury of any kind might prove my undoing."

Lardner (or his spokesman whom he called Ring Lardner) had been hoping to buy his wife a new fur coat from the money he would win betting on the 1919 World's Series in baseball, but he had lost his bet then and now he was going to try again. As a matter of fact this hardened professional sportswriter always seemed to lose money on his bets, despite his inside sports savvy.

Poor Ellis Lardner, that is, if anyone really believed that Lardner's American missus was modeled on her, instead of being, like his American mister, a fictional folk figure of high accuracy and brilliance. What a takeoff there is in this sketch of women's fashions, fur coats, and fancy, snobbish clothing, as being among those emblems of social standing, position, and prestige described, by Thorstein Veblen, as we have seen, as items of "conspicuous consumption," or ostentatious display. When it looks as if he is going to lose his bet again, Lardner considers settling on a cat-skin coat, to be furnished by the little feline members in his home;

and then finally decides instead on a black and red and tan plush jacket, the material for which is to be supplied by his friends and readers tearing off the plush covers off their family albums and sending them to him.

"Thompson's Vacation" is another of the Lardnerian Dada plays, a little spoof on fun and games between competing tourists, that whole group of middle- and upper-middle-class Americans already mentioned, who try to outdo each other on where they have been and what they have done. The worst of them always bring home slides or movies of obscure countries in Asia, Africa, etc., which at that are better to look at for an evening than to listen to them describing the trip, as Lardner, more or less, would have said.

We have already discussed the Dada plays "Clemo Uti—'The Water Lilies'" and "I. Gaspiri (The Upholsterers)," both of which were published in *What of It?*. But "The Quadroon," which is included in *First and Last* is a late play, which first appeared in *The New Yorker* in December 1931. It is a take-off on Eugene O'Neill's epical drama, *Mourning Becomes Electra*. O'Neill's work is a trilogy, consisting of "Homecoming," "The Hunted," and "The Haunted," in which the ancient Greek *Oresteia* of Aeschylus is brought up to date, so to speak, in a New England seaport town after the Civil War. It took either an afternoon and an evening, or two full afternoons, to see the O'Neill opus (it is still one of the major dramatic achievements of the American stage), and Lardner's four-part parody of it, "Hic," "Haec," "Hoc," and "Hujus," is mainly concerned with the luncheon and dinner menus that the O'Neill audience would have to look at in the intermissions between the plays.

But the dialogue in Lardner's "The Quadroon" pales when compared with that in another of these Dada plays called "Dinner Bridge." The scene there is a section of the Fifty-ninth Street Bridge in New York City which has been torn up for repair (the play's point is that one part or another of the road on this bridge, which leads directly to Queens and thence to Long Island, is always torn up for repair). The laborers are busy breaking up the pavement, a concrete mixer is standing by, when two waiters enter, in formal dress, bearing trays with cocktails and canapés. "The laborers cease their work and consume these appetizers. The noon whistle blows. The waiters bring in a white table cloth. . . ." Dinner is announced, and the men escort each other very formally to the table which has place cards on it. After all the dinner rituals have been settled, one of the workmen, Amorosi, says that he has been married twice: ". . . My first wife died."

HANSEN: How long were you married to her?

AMOROSI: Right up to the time she died.

CHAMALES, *interrupting:* Mr. Amorosi, you said you had been married twice.

AMOROSI: Yes, sir. My second wife was a Swiss girl.

HANSEN: Is she here with you?

AMOROSI: No, she's in Switzerland, in jail. She turned out to be a murderer.

CROWLEY: When it's a woman, you call her a murderess.

TAYLOR: And when it's a Swiss woman, you call her a Swiss-ess.

And so on, in an elaborate parody of high-toned dinner conversation among the laborers who are endlessly repairing the Fifty-ninth Street Bridge—laborers who are so cultivated, such gentlemen, and who obviously don't work very hard, just as in "A Yacht Race" the international competitors for the famous America Cup never got started, or in effect went backward. What comic visions of frustration and futility Lardner's imagination threw out, when they were not morbid or tragic. In "Cora, or Fun at a Spa, *An Expressionist Drama of Love and Death and Sex*——" Lardner both acknowledged his connection with the Expressionist (and Dadaistic) artistic movement of despair—and what we now call black comedy—and made a parody of it. The cast of characters includes "A Friend of the President; Plague Bennett, an Embryo Steeplejack; Elsa, their ward; the Manager of the Pump Room; Mrs. Tyler; and a Man Who Looks a Good Deal like Heywood Broun" (the newspaper columnist we have mentioned). The scene of Act I is

A pharmacy at a Spa. The Proprietor is at present out of the city and Mrs. Tyler is taking his place. She is a woman who seems to have been obliged to leave school while in the eighth grade. Plague Bennett enters. His mother named him Plague as tribute to her husband, who died of it. . . .

There is some highly surrealistic and nonsensical dialogue between Plague and Mrs. Tyler and the Friend of the President. Act II then takes place in "*a poultry yard at a Spa*":

The chairs and tables are in disarray as if a blotter salesman had been making his rounds. The Manager of the Pump Room is out of the city and the poultry are being fed by Mrs. Tyler. A Dead Ringer for David Belasco enters, crosses stage.

David Belasco was a famous Broadway producer and theatrical figure of Lardner's period, and Mrs. Tyler says to his double affectionately, "You old master you!" while in an aside, she comments: "I can never tell whether he's in first speed or reverse." The Manager of the Pump Room returns unexpectedly from out of town and asks, "I wonder what is keeping Elsa." He looks toward the right stage, and adds, "Ah! There she comes now, dancing as usual." But Elsa enters from the left of the stage, "fooling him completely," Lardner says. "She is not even dancing. She looks as if she had taken a bath."

Lardner had the habit, as we know, of including the real names of his contemporaries in his work, and the next of these little plays in *First and Last*, called "Abend Di Anni Nouveau," contains among the listed characters (new characters, or unheard-of ones, often made their appearance in a Lardner Dada play) the writer St. John Ervine as an immigrant, the columnist Walter Winchell as a nun, Heywood Broun as an usher at Roxy's (the New York movie theater); the columnist Dorothy Thompson as a football tackle, Theodore Dreiser as a former Follies girl, H. L. Mencken as "a kleagle in Moose," the Chicago writer Ben Hecht as a taxi starter, the movie mogul Carl Laemmle as "toys and games, sporting goods, outing flannels." Jeopardy. Two snail-gunders enter from the right, riding a tricycle. They shout their wares":

FIRST SNAIL-GUNDER: Wares! Wares!
A NEWSBOY: 'Wares who?
FIRST SNAIL-GUNDER: Anybody. That is, anybody who wants their snails gunded.

In the last act—"Acts 3, 4, and 5"—Lardner's stage directions read: *Three men suddenly begin to giggle. It is a secret, but they give the impression that one of them's mother runs a waffle parlor. They go off the stage still giggling. Two Broadway theatrical producers, riding pelicans, enter almost nude.*" One of these producers asks the other, "Have you got a dime?" and the other answers, "What do you think I am, a stage hand?" So much for the enchanted world of show business, now viewed in a more comic light. The last of the Lardnerian Dada plays, called "Taxidea Americana: A Play in Six Acts, Transplanted from the Mastoid by Ring W. Lardner," includes such characters as "Fred Rullman, an acorn huckster; Old Chloe, their colored mammy; Thomas Gregory, a poltroon; Mrs. Gregory, his mother, afterward his wife; Phoebe, engaged to Chloe; Professor Schwartz, instructor in Swiss at Wisconsin; Buddy, their daughter." Here again, Acts 2 and 4 were left out through an oversight, and Act 5 was located at Camp Randall, "just before the annual game between Wisconsin and the Wilmerding School for the Blind." There is "the Wisconsin battle hymn," a parody of college songs:

CHORUS

Far above Cayuga's waters with its waves of
blue
On Wisconsin, Minnesota and Bully for old
Purdue.
Notre Dame we yield to thee! Ohio State,
hurrah!
We'll drink a cup o' kindness yet in praise
of auld Nassau!

And the Wilmerding School for the Blind replies with its anthem:

CHORUS

We are always there on time!
We are the Wilmerding School for the Blind!
Better backfield, better line!
We are the Wilmerding School for the Blind!
Yea!

And thus we come to Ring Lardner's last song in the present account of his life and work. The class is over; school is out; and we must turn to more serious things. Now I know some readers may be wondering why I have chosen to end this account on the note of Lardner's nonsense comedy after all the tragedy and suffering in his short life, his last years of illness, his premature and painful death. But Ring Lardner would know why, I think, and would approve. A whole line of American humorists, rising in our Midwestern States after the Civil War, have reminded us that the only way to endure the pain and tragedy of life— that you who are young yet, and innocent and happy, will also have to meet when your time comes—that the only way to meet and endure life itself gracefully and completely is through the divine gift of laughter, of humor, of wit and the comic sense.

Without this one is helpless indeed—and as Mark Twain said, if death is the one true gift of life, the human race has never yet truly understood the power of laughter to meet and to overcome our pain and suffering, the series of small deaths we all suffer in life. That is all we really have to survive with in a universe that so often appears blind, dark, and indifferent to human existence: this gift of life, light, and laughter which all the great writers, tragic and comic alike, know to be the only meaning of our days on earth. If this study of Ring Lardner has contributed to that lesson, and you truly understand it a little better, that is all that any book can do. At least, that is what I hope this book has done, in some small measure.

A SELECTED BIBLIOGRAPHY

By Ring Lardner

You Know Me Al. New York: George H. Doran, 1916

Gullible's Travels. Indianapolis: Bobbs-Merrill Co., 1917

The Young Immigrunts. Indianapolis: Bobbs-Merrill Co., 1920

The Big Town. Indianapolis: Bobbs-Merrill Co., 1921

Symptoms of Being 35. Indianapolis: Bobbs-Merrill Co., 1921

Say It with Oil. New York: George H. Doran, 1923

How to Write Short Stories. New York: Charles Scribner's Sons, 1924

What of It? New York: Charles Scribner's Sons, 1925

The Love Nest and Other Stories. New York: Charles Scribner's Sons, 1926

The Story of a Wonder Man. New York: Charles Scribner's Sons, 1927

Round Up. New York: Charles Scribner's Sons, 1929

June Moon, with George S. Kaufman. New York: Charles Scribner's Sons, 1930

Lose with a Smile. New York: Charles Scribner's Sons, 1933

First and Last, edited by Gilbert Seldes. New York: Charles Scribner's Sons, 1934

The Collected Short Stories of Ring Lardner. New York: Modern Library, 1941

The Portable Ring Lardner, edited by Gilbert Seldes. New York: Viking Press, 1946

Shut Up, He Explained, edited by Babette Rosmond and

Henry Morgan. New York: Charles Scribner's Sons, 1962

The Ring Lardner Reader, edited by Maxwell Geismar. New York: Charles Scribner's Sons, 1963

About Ring Lardner

Ring Lardner: A Biography, Donald Elder. New York: Doubleday & Co., 1956

INDEX

ABOUT THE AUTHOR

Maxwell Geismar received his B.A. from Columbia College and his M.A. from Columbia University. The author of many books, including *Writers in Crisis, The Last of the Provincials, Rebels and Ancestors, American Moderns, Henry James and the Jacobites,* and *Mark Twain: An American Prophet,* he has also edited a number of volumes, among them a collection of Ring Lardner's prose, poems, and plays, *The Ring Lardner Reader.*

Mr. Geismar has been interested in Lardner for the past thirty years. Although in that time he has written about a score of other American writers, he says "Lardner has always been a favorite author in our house from the time I read such essays as *The Young Immigrunts* to our children, who grew up 'laughing on Lardner.' " Mr. Geismar taught Lardner for twelve years to his students at Sarah Lawrence College. An essay about Lardner, which he wrote in 1941, led to the publication a year later of Mr. Geismar's first book—*Writers in Crisis.*

Mr. Geismar lives with his wife in Harrison, New York.